MW00803065

A South Carolina Chronology

THIRD EDITION

A SOUTH CAROLINA CHRONOLOGY

THIRD EDITION

Walter Edgar, J. Brent Morris, and
C. James Taylor

THE UNIVERSITY OF
SOUTH CAROLINA PRESS

© 2020 University of South Carolina

Published by the University of South Carolina Press
Columbia, South Carolina 29208

www.uscpress.com

Manufactured in the United States of America

29 28 27 26 25 24 23 22 21 20
10 9 8 7 6 5 4 3 2 1

Library of Congress Cataloging-in-Publication Data
can be found at http://catalog.loc.gov/.

ISBN: 978-1-64336-164-2 (hardcover)
ISBN: 978-1-64336-165-9 (paperback)
ISBN: 978-1-64336-166-6 (ebook)

CONTENTS

Preface   vii

I. Peopling the Continent (17,200 BCE–1669)   1

II. The Colony (1670–1764)   9

III. Revolution (1765–1790)   32

IV. South Carolina and the Union (1791–1859)   53

V. Secession, Rebellion, and Redemption (1860–1895)   80

VI. A Segregated South Carolina (1896–1964)   99

VII. A Changing South Carolina (1965–1999)   123

VIII. Modern South Carolina (2000–2020)   142

Index   155

This modest book contains the principal events, developments, and dates in the history of South Carolina. It is our intention to have incorporated events that would reflect the total history of the province and the state such that one reading the full volume would be aware of the fundamental developments in Carolina society and the major changes that have occurred.

This third edition of *A South Carolina Chronology* has been necessitated by the passage of nearly three decades and changes that have occurred in the focus and direction of American historiography over that time. In addition to the new broader reading of events that expands the previously chronicled period to take more notice of race, gender, and other social issues, a generation of notable changes and remarkable events have added measurably to South Carolina's history and this chronology.

We fully anticipate that this work will be updated again in the future, perhaps by a new generation of historians who may read this Chronology as their first survey of South Carolina's rich past. The focus almost certainly will have changed, and historians will be asking new questions. Without a doubt, readers will note omissions, some likely significant. Another generation of the state's history will need to be chronicled. And so, as was the case in the 1973 and 1994 editions, we invite readers to report errors and omissions to be kept on file for that inevitable revision.

Peopling the Continent
(17,200 BCE–1669)

The foothills and coastal plain bounded on the south by the Savannah River, on the west by the Appalachian Mountains, and on the east by the Atlantic Ocean, make up the territory we now call South Carolina. The state has no major natural boundary to the north until one comes to the Roanoke River, which empties into the Albemarle Sound around latitude 36 north. The region is divided into a geologically very ancient area of Precambrian rock formations, of which the blue granite quarried in Fairfield County is an example, and a flat southeastern area where sand, shells, and marl were deposited in the relatively recent Cretaceous period.

We know very little about the Indigenous people who lived here before European settlement. Each year new archeological discoveries are made, and we learn more about the first inhabitants of this region. Most scholars subscribe to the Beringean land mass theory in which humans followed migrations of large game across the Bering Sea land bridge around 20,000 years ago from Asia to North America. These were the ancestors of Incas, Mayans, Aztecs, Iroquois, Cherokee, Catawbas, and all Native American tribes that have figured in the history of what is now the United States and of South Carolina. One feature of their cultures shared throughout the inhabited "new world" was the building of mounds for ceremonial and religious purposes. The most exciting remains are the temples of Central America, and dozens of these earthen formations remain intact with the boundaries of present-day South Carolina.

The major pre-Columbian Indigenous groups in what has become the state of South Carolina were the Iroquoian, Algonquian, Muskogean, Siouan, and Cusabo peoples. At the time of the entrance of the Europeans—Spanish, French, and English—the native inhabitants had organized themselves into chiefdoms with both significant degrees of democracy and elaborate noble hierarchies, the Cacique of Kiawah and the Queen of Confitachiqui being the best-known examples.

Europeans, though still recovering from the catastrophic Bubonic Plague of the 14th century, began to cast a curious gaze westward over the ocean in the next century. Before the end of the 15th century, explorers had stumbled upon a new continent, encountered its inhabitants, and begun attempts to colonize it. The Spanish and Portuguese spread across South, Central America, and southern North America, while the English established a foothold on North America's Atlantic Seaboard, south of the French colonial projects to their north.

In the region which would become South Carolina, Native Americans, Europeans, and the enslaved Africans they had brought with them negotiated a world which was, in every way, new for them all.

17,200 BCE

Ancient Indigenous people were present at the "Topper site" in Allendale County. They visited this area to collect Allendale Coastal Plain chert, a prized stone for use in the making of projectile points. Artifacts collected at this site established a pre-Clovis human presence in the area, with some controversial estimates pushing the earliest date of habitation back tens of thousands of years earlier.

8,000–1,500 BCE

Humans during the Archaic Horizon era created shell mounds and middens along the Atlantic coast.

2,500–1,000 BCE

Humans living along the Savannah River were producing fiber-tempered pottery.

1,000 BCE–1,500 CE

People of the Woodland period began to settle down, domesticate plants, create sophisticated pottery, and hunt with bows and arrows, in addition to spears. South Carolina's Woodland people included Siouan people living in the area east of the Catawba/

Wateree rivers and north of the Santee; Muskogean south of the Santee, along the coast to Savannah; Iroquoian in the western third of the state; and Algonquian along the Savannah between Iroquoian and Muskogean territories.

1,150 CE

Mississippian people entered South Carolina and built a series of settlements in river valleys along the fall zone. The Mississippian chiefdom of Cofitachequi established its capital at Mulberry Mound on the Wateree River (Kershaw County).

1491

The Indigenous population of the region which would become South Carolina before European contact was likely somewhere between 17,000 and 30,000.

1497

John Cabot sailed from Bristol for North America on May 20, made his landfall near the northern tip of Newfoundland on June 24, and returned to Bristol on August 6. By this remarkably swift voyage, England claimed title of all of North America by right of discovery.

1514–1516

In search of slaves Capt. Pedro de Salazar, an agent of Santo Domingo planter Lucas Vasquez de Ayllon sailed north, past the Bahama islands, and made landfall somewhere on the coast of present-day South Carolina. He captured 500 Indigenous people, two-thirds of whom died on the voyage back to Hispaniola.

1521

JUNE

Lucas Vasquez de Ayllon sent an expedition from Santo Domingo, captained by Francisco Gordillo, which explored the Florida coast as far north as thirty-three degrees thirty minutes, thereby making a claim in the name of the king of Spain to an area which would have included present-day Carolina. Back in Spain, "Francisco el Chicorano," one of the men enslaved by Gordillo, regaled audiences with tales of his homeland which were later published by the chronicler Peter Martyr.

1524

Giovanni da Verrazzano, commissioned by the king of France to explore the New World, sighted land in March just north of present-day Myrtle Beach before sailing northward in quest of the western sea.

1526

Ayllón, now Governor and Captain General of La Florida, established the first European settlement in what is now South Carolina at San Miguel de Gualdape, which scholars place somewhere along the coast of present-day South Carolina. The Spaniards called the land Chicora. The initial population of the settlement was approximately 600, including a number of enslaved people from Santo Domingo.

OCTOBER 18

After a short illness, likely dysentery, Ayllón died, followed by a leadership struggle among the European survivors and a strike on the village by a local Indigenous group.

NOVEMBER

The enslaved people at San Miguel de Gualdape mutinied. This was the first slave revolt in North America. Disheartened by disease, famine, the death of their leader, the slave revolt, and an unusually severe winter, the surviving settlers left San Miguel. About 150 of them reached Santo Domingo.

1540

APRIL

Coming from the south, Hernando de Soto crossed the Savannah River into the interior of present-day South Carolina and encountered an Indigenous chiefdom called Confitachiqui. Archaeologists believe the main settlement was located near present-day Camden, just below the fall line on the Wateree River.

MAY 3

DeSoto left Confitachiqui and made his way across the mountains, probably by way of the French Broad and Tennessee rivers.

1562

MAY

Jean Ribaut and a group of French Huguenots planted a settlement, which he called Charlesfort, on Parris Island. He named the region Carolus in honor of Charles IX of France and gave the name Port Royal to the sound that still bears that name.

JUNE 11

Ribaut sailed home, leaving behind about thirty men who soon became desperate. Believing themselves to have been forgotten, they sailed to Europe in a makeshift vessel and were forced to turn to cannibalism when food ran out.

1564

JUNE 22

Rene de Laudonnière and a second group of Huguenots landed in Florida. A few days later they settled near the mouth of the St. John's River and built Fort Caroline.

1565

SEPTEMBER 8

The Spaniard Pedro Menéndez de Avilés took possession of the first site of St. Augustine, Florida, which became the center of Spanish influence south of Carolina and, in the eighteenth century, the great rival of Charles Town.

SEPTEMBER 29

Menéndez massacred the French after the capture of Fort Caroline.

1566

APRIL

Menéndez ordered built the Spanish outpost known as Fort San Felipe at Santa Elena on Parris Island, the former site of Charlesfort.

NOVEMBER

Menéndez sent Juan Pardo to explore the hinterland of Fort San Felipe. Pardo reached the mountains. He leads a second exploratory voyage into the interior in 1567.

1571

JULY

Santa Elena designated the capital of La Florida on the arrival and establishment of residence of Pedro Menéndez and his family.

1576

JULY

Native Americans attacked Fort San Felipe and Santa Elena and forced the Spaniards to retreat to St. Augustine.

1577

The Spaniards returned to build Fort San Marcos not far from where Fort San Felipe had stood at Santa Elena. Spanish missions, along the coast from St. Augustine as far north at least as the South Edisto River, survived until 1686.

1629

OCTOBER 30

Charles I of England granted to his attorney general Sir Robert Heath the territory in America between thirty-one and thirty-six degrees north latitude. This land, which extended from the northern limits of modern Florida to Albemarle Sound and from ocean to ocean, was to be called Carolana in honor of King Charles I.

1663

MARCH 24

Charles II granted the territory which had been called Carolana to loyal political allies Edward Hyde (Earl of Clarendon), George Monck (Duke of Albemarle), William Craven (Earl of Craven), John Berkeley (Baron Berkeley of Stratton), Anthony Ashley Cooper (Baron Ashley of Wimborne St. Giles), Sir George Carteret, Sir William Berkeley, and Sir John Colleton, who were designated "the true and absolute Lords Proprietors" of what was now to be known as Carolina.

AUGUST 26

Capt. William Hilton, who had sailed from Barbados on August 10 to explore the new grant in the names of the Lords Proprietors, reached the coast of Carolina and probed the creeks and rivers around the island now called Hilton Head. He returned to Barbados on January 6, 1664.

1664

MAY 29

The Barbadians made a short-lived settlement on the Cape Fear River within the Carolina tract. Sir John Yeamans was appointed governor of this colony, the county of Clarendon.

1665

JANUARY 7

The *Concessions and Agreements* between the Lords Proprietors and William Yeamans, the son of Sir John, and others contained provisions for governing and distributing land in Carolina.

JUNE 30

A second charter was granted to the Lords Proprietors of Carolina in order to remove a possible defect in their title. The new boundaries reached as far north as the present Virginia–North Carolina line and as far south as 100 miles below the present Georgia–Florida line.

1666

JUNE 14–JULY 12

Capt. Robert Sandford, Secretary and Chief Register of the county of Clarendon (Cape Fear settlement), at the direction of Gov. Yeamans explored the coast to the south of Cape Fear.

1667

AUTUMN

The county of Clarendon was abandoned.

1669

MARCH 1

The Eight Lords Proprietors adopted the Fundamental Constitutions of Carolina. The document was heavily influenced by the ideas of Anthony Ashley Cooper's secretary John Locke and perhaps by those of James Harrington. The adventurous settlers never accepted this or later versions of the Fundamental Constitutions, which are, however, generally felt to have influenced the character of the state as it developed. The Constitutions decreed that most governmental power would be in the hands of a landed gentry, for whom various titles were specified. This first version allowed an unusually large degree of religious toleration.

AUGUST

The ships *Carolina, Port Royal,* and *Albemarle* sailed from England with 100 colonists under the command of Joseph West, who later emerged as the ablest of the early leaders of the colony, serving as governor three times.

SEPTEMBER 17

Soon after this date the three ships left Kinsale, Ireland, where additional settlers had been taken on.

LATE OCTOBER

The three ships reached Barbados.

NOVEMBER 2

A storm wrecked the *Albemarle,* but the passengers and crew were rescued.

II

The Colony
(1670–1764)

After difficult beginnings, the settlement at Charles Town suddenly egan to boom when the pirates unloaded their loot and the settlers opened up a trade in skins and furs with the Native Americans. About the same time (1685–1696) the terms "South Carolina" and "North Carolina" came into use. Although the two settlements were formally part of the same "Carolina" province, they were not only hundreds of miles apart (one around Albemarle Sound and the other at Charles Town) but also were culturally very different from each other, and it was never practicable to administer them as one unit. North Carolina's early settlers were mostly immigrants from Virginia, and the coast north of Cape Fear was lacking in natural harbors. For a time (1692–1710) North Carolina was governed by deputies appointed by the governors of South Carolina who resided in Charles Town. North Carolina's prosperity came only later once the hinterland was developed.

South Carolina's early prosperity was bought at a terrible price. Greed overcame the moral scruples that some settlers surely had about owning other people as slaves. Enslaved people, imported at first from Barbados and then directly from Africa, were found to be more tractable workers (and indeed, more knowledgeable) in the rice fields after that crop was introduced in the 1690s and more resistant to malaria than Native Americans. By 1708 the number of Africans in the colony exceeded the number of whites and by 1730, excluding Native Americans, Africans constituted two-thirds of the population. After 1750, because of white immigration overland from Pennsylvania and Virginia, the proportion of whites in the population increased until the 1790s when the white population was again the majority.

Besides deerskin and rice, ships' supplies (naval stores) such as lumber, tar, and turpentine were also exported profitably. By the late 1740s indigo had become an important export, but cotton was not a significant crop until the 1790s.

During this period Charles Town became one of the wealthiest towns in North America, with a sophisticated social and cultural life, although it never acquired the official English status of a city. By 1735 Beaufort and Georgetown had become substantial settlements and were able to compete with Charles Town for trade.

1670

JANUARY 12

The *Port Royal* was wrecked in the Bahamas.

FEBRUARY

Sir John Yeamans appointed Col. William Sayle of Bermuda as the first governor of Carolina. Sayle was seventy-nine years old when he began his term March 17.

FEBRUARY 26

Under command of Sayle, the *Carolina* and a newly acquired vessel, the *Three Brothers,* left Bermuda for the Carolina coast with instructions from the Proprietors to establish a settlement at Port Royal.

MARCH 1

In England, the second version of the Fundamental Constitutions was drawn up. It was not ratified.

MARCH 15

The settlers sighted land near Bulls Bay.

APRIL

After exploring the coast southward to Port Royal Sound the settlers, at the suggestion of a local Indian chief, the Cacique of Kiawah, fixed upon Albemarle Point up the Ashley River for their first home.

SUMMER

The first public elections were held in Carolina for membership in the Council.

AUGUST 23

Capt. Henry Brayne brought the first enslaved Africans to English Carolina.

AUGUST

A Spanish attempt from St. Augustine to destroy the new English settlement failed. By the end of 1670, word reached America of the Treaty of Madrid (July 18, 1670), in which Spain recognized the existence of English settlements north of St. Augustine. The estimated population of the settlement was 155, of whom about 15 were African. The Native American population of what we now call South Carolina was probably between 20,000 and 50,000.

1671

Stephen Bull sent a roll of South Carolina–grown tobacco to the Proprietors.

JULY

South Carolina's first assembly, called a parliament, met.

1672

JANUARY 13

The Lords Proprietors sent a barrel of rice with other supplies aboard the *William & Ralph*. This may have been used as seed and marked the beginning of rice cultivation in South Carolina that would prosper after the 1680s with the introduction of Madagascar rice.

APRIL 23

In England, Lord Ashley was named the first Earl of Shaftesbury.

1674

OCTOBER

Dr. Henry Woodward forged an alliance with the Westo Indians that opened a lucrative trade in skins and enslaved Indians until a war dampened relations in 1680.

1679

DECEMBER 17

The Lords Proprietors ordered the site of the settlement to be moved from Albemarle Point to Oyster Point, which lay at the confluence of the Ashley and Cooper rivers, and to be named Charles Town.

1680

The estimated population of the colony, excluding Native Americans, was 1,200 including approximately 200 enslaved Africans.

APRIL 30

The first group of Huguenots arrived at Oyster Point in the *Richmond.*

1681

English Congregationalists, Scots and Irish Presbyterians, and French Huguenots of the original Charles Town settlement founded a dissenting congregation called the Independent Church. Their first church building, known as the White Meeting House, gave Meeting Street its name.

1682

St. Philip's congregation organized with its first church erected at the current site of St. Michael's in Charles Town.

JANUARY 12

In England, the third version of the Fundamental Constitutions was drawn up. It was not ratified.

MAY 10

The Lords Proprietors ordered three counties to be laid out: Craven to the north, Berkeley in the center, Colleton to the south.

AUGUST 17

In England, the fourth version of the Fundamental Constitutions was drawn up. It was not ratified.

1683

DECEMBER 23

Quaker leader George Fox addressed a letter to the Friends of Charles Town on Ashley Cooper River in Carolina. This is the first evidence of Quaker activity in South Carolina.

1684

MARCH

The first Baptist congregation settled in South Carolina (on the Cooper River near Charles Town) after fleeing Massachusetts.

NOVEMBER

A group of Scots, covenanters who had not fared well under the Restoration, settled Stuart's Town near present-day Beaufort.

1685

FEBRUARY 6

In England, James II ascended the throne. Thereafter royal authority became more evident in the colonies. Apparently rice was being grown commercially in Carolina, and George Muschamp, the first direct representative of royal authority in the colony, came to collect customs and enforce the Navigation Acts.

OCTOBER 18

In France, Louis XIV revoked the Edict of Nantes, which had guaranteed the rights of Huguenots. About 1,500 of them emigrated to South Carolina in the next ten years.

1686

AUGUST 17

The Spanish destroyed Stuart's Town.

1687

The Huguenot Church in Charles Town was organized.

1688

DECEMBER

In England, "The Glorious Revolution" caused James II to flee to France.

1689

Albemarle County ceased to function as a governmental unit. Chowan, Currituck, Pasquotank, and Perquimans precincts became recognized as counties, and the government of Carolina "north and east of Cape Fear" was established.

DECEMBER 16

Parliament enacted the English Bill of Rights, which had been accepted by William and Mary previously on February 13.

1690

FEBRUARY 7

South Carolina enacted its first law relating solely to slavery.

SEPTEMBER 20

The South Carolina Grand Council granted a patent to Peter Jacob Guerard for his pendulum engine that husked rice.

NOVEMBER 8

The Lords Proprietors commissioned Phillip Ludwell as governor of all "Carolina." By the end of this year it was the practice, sanctioned by the Lords Proprietors, for the Grand Council to meet in two houses, one of deputies appointed by the Proprietors and the other of representatives elected by the people. Thus began the bicameral legislature.

DECEMBER

A parliament convened in Charles Town banished the tyrannical and inept governor James Colleton. He was succeeded by Seth Sothell, who had previously been governor in North Carolina.

1692

APRIL

Phillip Ludwell arrived in Charles Town and appointed a deputy to govern "north and east of Cape Fear." The northern colony continued to be governed by deputies from Charles Town until 1710.

1693

MAY 11

The Lords Proprietors declared the Fundamental Constitutions inoperative—a formal recognition of the colonists' refusal to implement the system.

1695

AUGUST 17

Quaker John Archdale became governor and inaugurated a period of sound and relatively popular government.

LATE AUGUST

Archdale documents the first Jewish Carolinian, his Spanish interpreter.

DECEMBER 5

A group of New Englanders left Dorchester, Massachusetts, for a place on the Ashley River which they named Dorchester. They celebrated their arrival with divine service on January 26, 1696.

1696

MARCH 16

South Carolina enacted its first comprehensive slave law. It was based on the Barbados slave code of 1688.

1698

The Society for the Propagation of Christian Knowledge established a parochial library in Charles Town.

FEBRUARY 24

A fire destroyed at least fifty structures in Charles Town, a third of the urban area. The Commons House of Assembly later enacted a special fire code in October 1698.

APRIL 11

In England, the fifth and final version of the Fundamental Constitutions was drawn up. It was not ratified.

OCTOBER 8

Afraid of the growing number of Africans who had been imported as slaves, the Commons House of Assembly passed a law granting £13 to anyone who would bring into the province a white male servant.

1699

Benjamin Simons built Middleburg, the oldest house still standing in South Carolina, on the Eastern Branch of the Cooper River.

AUGUST 29–NOVEMBER 1

Nearly 200 people died in the first confirmed yellow fever epidemic.

1700

The estimated population of the province, excluding Native Americans, was 5,500. The population of enslaved Africans is not known but was probably about 2,400.

NOVEMBER 16

The Commons House of Assembly voted a financial contribution to the Charles Town parochial library, thus making it the first public library in the country.

1702

MAY

Queen Anne's War began an eleven-year struggle against France and Spain for power in North America. Word of the war's outbreak did not reach South Carolina until August 26.

NOVEMBER–DECEMBER

Gov. James Moore attacked St. Augustine. He failed to take the fort but burned the town.

DECEMBER 25

The Reverend Samuel Thomas, the first missionary sent out by the recently established Society for the Propagation of the Gospel in Foreign Parts, reached Charles Town.

1703

MAY 6

In order to break up the brisk trade in enslaved Native Americans, the Commons House of Assembly placed a duty of twenty shillings per head on each such slave exported. Many were exported to the West Indies and to New England.

MAY 8

The Commons House of Assembly issued bills of credit in the amount of £6,000 to pay for the war against Florida (the first "paper money" issued in the colony).

1704

A map by Edward Crisp showed Charles Town as a walled city. Charles Town, Santa Fe, and St. Augustine were the only walled cities ever erected within the confines of the present United States.

JANUARY

Former Gov. James Moore led his second expedition against Florida, attacking the Apalachees. Only four white Carolinians lost their lives, but Spanish territories were seriously weakened.

MAY 5

Payment was made for a Sword of State which was used by Proprietary, Royal, and State governments until it disappeared in 1941.

1705

SEPTEMBER 29

On this date Parliament placed rice on the list of enumerated
goods, which meant that all rice being shipped to Europe must pass
through an English port.

1706

SEPTEMBER 9–10

Despite an epidemic of yellow fever, Gov. Sir Nathaniel Johnson
and Col. William Rhett repulsed an attack on Charles Town by
French and Spanish forces marching from Bulls Bay to the Wando
River.

NOVEMBER 30

The Commons House of Assembly established the Church of
England in the province. The act divided the colony into ten parishes: St. Philip's, Christ Church, St. Thomas's and St. Denis's, St.
James's Santee, St. John's Berkeley, St. James's Goose Creek, St. Andrew's, St. Paul's, and St. Bartholomew's. A church was to be built
in each parish at public expense. The first to be built was that of
St. Andrew's, which was begun in 1706.

1707

Thomas Nairne, appointed Indian agent by the Commons House
of Assembly, attempted to direct an enlightened policy toward the
Native Americans. He was killed in the Yemassee War April 15, 1715.

Henrietta Dering Johnston, the first woman professional artist in
the colonies and the first pastel artist in America, arrived in Charles
Town.

MAY 1

The Act of Union between England and Scotland henceforth permitted Scots to settle and trade in Carolina on equal terms with the
English.

JULY 19

The Commons House of Assembly enacted "An Act for Regulating the Indian Trade and Making it Safe to the Publick" and placed the Indian trade under the control of nine commissioners appointed by the Commons House of Assembly.

OCTOBER 25

Land grants reveal that by this date what had been Port Royal County was now known as Granville County. It extended along the north side of the Savannah River far into the backcountry.

1708

SEPTEMBER 17

Gov. Sir Nathaniel Johnson reported population figures that revealed a Black majority in South Carolina for the first time.

Enslaved African	4,100
White	4,080
Enslaved Indian	1,400
Total	9,580

DECEMBER 7

The Lords Proprietors decided to appoint a governor for North Carolina who would be "independent of the governor of Carolina." Edward Hyde became first governor of North Carolina in 1712. Henceforth, North Carolina was governed as a separate colony.

1711

JANUARY 17

The Lords Proprietors ordered that the town of Beaufort on Port Royal Sound be established to serve as an outlet for the naval stores produced in Granville and Colleton counties.

DECEMBER

Col. John Barnwell led an expedition into North Carolina which suppressed an uprising of the Tuscarora Indians. He would return the following June having earned the nickname "Tuscarora Jack."

1712

JUNE 7

The Commons House of Assembly laid out the Parish of St. Helena to contain all of Granville County.

DECEMBER

Col. James Moore, son of the former governor, led a second expedition against the Tuscaroras of North Carolina. He would decisively defeat them by March 1713.

DECEMBER 12

The Commons House of Assembly enacted a statute formally adopting the English common law and 126 named English statutes selected by Chief Justice Nicholas Trott.

DECEMBER 12

The Commons House of Assembly passed legislation to establish a free school in Charles Town-the beginning of public education in South Carolina.

1715

APRIL 15

The massacre of almost 100 white settlers near Port Royal began the Yemassee War. The white settlers, with the aid of forces that included free Native Americans, enslaved Africans, and reinforcements from North Carolina, quelled an uprising of the Yemassees, Cheraws, Creeks, Shawnees, and other tribes, which had jeopardized the safety of the colony.

1716

JANUARY 31

A 300-man military force marched into Cherokee territory to gain their support against the Creeks. The result was the first treaty with the Cherokees, who became indispensable allies of the settlers against the Creeks.

DECEMBER 15

The Commons House of Assembly passed legislation which designated the parishes, instead of the counties, as the units for representation in the Assembly. The law was disallowed in England.

1717

Sir Robert Montgomery, who had conceived of the establishment of the Margravate of Azilia as a buffer to the southward of Carolina, published in London *A Discourse Concerning the deign'd Establishment of a New Colony to the South of Carolina, in the Most delightful Country of the Universe.*

MAY 22

Edward Thatch (Teach), the notorious pirate Blackbeard, threatened to murder several prisoners and destroy Charles Town to coerce officials into sending him a chest of medicine.

NOVEMBER

A treaty signed in Charles Town with the Lower Creeks formally ended the Yemassee War.

DECEMBER 11

The Parish of St. George's Dorchester was carved out of St. Andrew's.

1718

Congaree Fort, the first frontier post in central South Carolina, was established.

SEPTEMBER 27

Col. William Rhett defeated the pirate ships of the notorious "gentleman pirate" Stede Bonnet in the Battle of Cape Fear River. Rhett transported prisoners to Charles Town to await charges of piracy. Stede Bonnet, who briefly escaped his confinement, was recaptured and hanged at White Point between high and low tide December 10.

OCTOBER 17

The Assembly passed an act for the more speedy and regular trial of pirates to punish them quickly.

1719

DECEMBER 10

The first step in the Revolution of 1719 (in which the Carolinians overthrew Proprietary rule) was taken when the Commons House of Assembly transformed itself into a convention of the people.

DECEMBER 21

The convention proclaimed James Moore (son of the earlier governor) their new governor in place of the Proprietors' appointee Robert Johnson.

1720

The estimated population of the colony, excluding Native Americans, was 18,500, of whom nearly 12,000 were enslaved Africans.

Col. John ("Tuscarora Jack") Barnwell was sent to England to speak for those who were now in power.

FEBRUARY 12

An act, the text of which has been lost, created the system of courts which lasted until the eve of the Revolution.

AUGUST 11

The Privy Council in England assumed responsibility for the government of South Carolina and appointed Francis Nicholson as the first royal governor.

1721

SEPTEMBER 2

A new act merged the militia and slave patrols, made policing slavery the militia's number one priority, and empowered watchmen to stop African Americans on sight. The statewide patrol system that remained in effect until the Civil War evolved from this legislation.

SEPTEMBER 19

The Commons House of Assembly passed a new election law which again divided the representation among the parishes. The law established a property qualification for voting of a fifty-acre freehold or twenty shillings paid in taxes. This remained the basic election law for the remainder of the colonial period until the American Revolution.

SEPTEMBER 20

The Commons House of Assembly, at the recommendation of Gov. Francis Nicholson, created the province's first county courts, thus establishing South Carolina's first courts outside of Charles Town. They did not, however, last the decade.

1722

MARCH 10

The Parish of Prince George Winyah was carved out of St. James Santee.

MARCH 25

Easter Day services were held for the first time in the new St. Philip's Church.

MAY 3

Mark Catesby, the naturalist, landed in Charles Town. At the direction of Sir Hans Sloane, founder of the British Museum, Catesby explored the backcountry and the Bahamas before returning to England in 1726. He published *The Natural History of Carolina, Florida, and the Bahama Islands* in two volumes (1731, 1743).

JUNE 23

The Commons House of Assembly passed a law to incorporate Charles Town and rename it Charles City and Port, but it was disallowed in England.

1725

DECEMBER 14

The Commons House of Assembly asserted its sole right to originate money bills and that the Council could only approve or reject such legislation.

1726

JUNE 26

After a brief flurry of interest by the Proprietors in reestablishing their control of South Carolina, the Privy Council concluded the province should remain under royal control.

1727

JUNE

The followers of the second Landgrave Thomas Smith, the leader of the anti-tax association in the northern parishes, marched on Charles Town.

1728

FEBRUARY

Col. John Palmer led an attack upon the Yemassee settlements near St. Augustine.

1729

On behalf of Elisha Screven, William Swinton laid out George Town on the banks of the Sampit River.

SEPTEMBER 29

The Lords Proprietors, with the exception of Lord Granville, formally surrendered their title and interest in Carolina for £2,500 sterling each.

NOVEMBER 30

The growing presence of the Scots in Charles Town was marked by the organization of the St. Andrew's Society.

1730

The estimated population of the colony, excluding Native Americans, was 30,000, of whom approximately two-thirds were enslaved Africans.

AUGUST 15

Charles Town authorities discovered an elaborate slave conspiracy that may have included as many as 200 participants. The ringleaders were immediately executed. This was the first slave conspiracy in British South Carolina to be detected.

SEPTEMBER 7

A treaty of friendship was signed in London between King George II and six Cherokee chiefs whom Sir Alexander Cuming had escorted to London. They had sailed from Charles Town on May 4 and returned with the new royal governor on December 15.

SEPTEMBER 29

After this date Parliament permitted vessels with licenses obtained in England to carry rice directly to European ports south of Cape Finisterre, Spain.

DECEMBER 15

Robert Johnson, the son of Sir Nathaniel Johnson and former governor under the Proprietors, arrived in Charles Town to assume the governorship of the new royal colony.

1731

AUGUST 20

A law establishing the royal quitrents put landholding on a secure and permanent basis. Registration of quitrents provided a permanent record of landholding.

AUGUST 20

A law stabilized the South Carolina paper currency on a ratio of seven to one with sterling. This exchange rate varied only slightly until the Revolution.

NOVEMBER 4

A printing press had been established by this date inasmuch as the first known South Carolina imprint, a proclamation of Gov. Johnson, was issued on this day.

1732

Jean Pierre Purry, a Swiss promoter, obtained 12,000 acres on the Savannah River and helped to transport over 600 immigrants to Purrysburg.

JANUARY 8

The first South Carolina newspaper, the *South-Carolina Gazette,* was published by Thomas Whitmarsh in Charles Town.

1733

JANUARY 13

James Oglethorpe arrived in Charles Town with the first settlers for Georgia.

FEBRUARY 12

Oglethorpe laid out the town of Savannah, Georgia, on Yamacraw Bluff on the Savannah River.

1734

APRIL 9

The Parish of St. John's Colleton was carved out of St. Paul's and the Parish of Prince Frederick out of Prince George Winyah.

1735

German Swiss immigrants began settlement in Orangeburg township.

Rhineland German immigrants began settling Saxe-Gotha township in modern Lexington County.

The governors of both Carolinas appointed a commission to survey the boundary between North Carolina and South Carolina.

FEBRUARY 18

The first opera performed in America, "Flora, or Hob in the Well," was staged in Charles Town.

1736

Nicholas Trott had Lewis Timothy publish in Charles Town his two-volume work, *The Laws of the Province of South Carolina.*

FEBRUARY 3

The Friendly Society for the Mutual Insuring of Houses against Fire organized in Charles Town (the first fire insurance company in America).

JULY 31

John Wesley made his first visit to Charles Town. He visited the city again April 14–23 and December 13–24, 1737. He sailed for England from Charles Town on December 24, 1737.

1737

The Boundary Commission completed the survey to define the boundary between North Carolina and South Carolina, which corresponded roughly to the modern boundary.

Welsh Baptists from Newcastle, Pennsylvania, settled in the Pee Dee region in what became known as the "Welsh Tract."

APRIL

Dr. John Lining began his meteorological observations and notations, the first recorded weather observations in America.

1738

A smallpox epidemic spread through the colony from a slave ship, infected more than two thousand of the roughly six thousand residents of Charles Town, and killed more than three hundred. It produced a controversy over the first known use of inoculation as a preventive measure in the colony.

1739

SEPTEMBER 9

Enslaved people from the Stono River plantations rose up in rebellion and marched toward St. Augustine, having heard that the Spaniards promised freedom. Forty Africans and twenty whites died in the insurrection.

DECEMBER 29

Charles Town printer Lewis Timothy died, and his wife Ann continued publishing the *South-Carolina Gazette*. She was America's first female printer.

1740

The estimated population of the colony, excluding Native Americans, was 60,000, of whom about two-thirds were enslaved Africans.

APRIL 5

After the Stono Rebellion the Commons House of Assembly greatly reduced the African slave trade by placing prohibitive taxes on the sale of recently imported enslaved laborers. The rate rose as high as £100 currency.

MAY 10

The Commons House of Assembly passed the Negro Act, a comprehensive series of laws for regulating the life and activities of enslaved Africans. This slave code endured with little change until the Civil War.

JULY 15

An ecclesiastical court held in St. Philip's Church accused Anglican clergyman the Rev. George Whitefield of conducting public services that did not follow the authorized forms of the Church of England Book of Common Prayer (Whitefield preached in Charles Town several times in 1740 and 1741). This trial was the beginning of a process that led to Whitefield's expulsion from the Church of England.

NOVEMBER 18

One of the most devastating of all Charles Town fires destroyed half the buildings in the town and bankrupted the Friendly Society for the Mutual Insuring of Houses.

1742

The Reverend Heinrich Melchior Muhlenberg visited Charles Town on his way from Ebenezer, Georgia, to Philadelphia and assisted in the establishment of the Lutheran Church in South Carolina.

SEPTEMBER 12

The Reverend Alexander Garden opened a school for Africans in Charles Town. The purpose was to train them "in the principles of Christianity and the fundamentals of education, to serve as schoolmasters to their people."

DECEMBER 17

James Glen arrived in Charles Town to assume the governorship. His term (until June 1, 1756) proved to be the longest of any South Carolina colonial governor.

1744

Eliza Lucas Pinckney proved that indigo could be grown in South Carolina, the equal of that grown by the French and Spaniards in the West Indies. She also used portions of her crop that year to make seed and shared it with other planters, leading to an expansion in indigo production in the region.

MARCH

King George's War began in Europe as the War of Austrian Succession.

JULY 23

Officials in Charles Town proclaimed war against France. Many Spanish and French ships were captured by the British Navy in the ensuing months and brought as prizes to Charles Town, including in December the 400-ton French ship *Conception,* estimated to be worth £80,000 sterling (including cargo).

1745

MAY 25

Prince William Parish was carved out of St. Helena's.

1747

FEBRUARY 17

The township of Purrysburg and adjacent parts were erected into the Parish of St. Peter.

1748

The English Parliament granted a six-pence-per pound bounty to the producers of Carolina indigo.

FEBRUARY 17–18

The temperature fell to ten degrees Fahrenheit, the coldest day in Charles Town in the eighteenth century. The intense cold killed the orange trees that for several years had produced enough fruit for export.

DECEMBER 28

The Charles Town Library Society organized on this date; the Commons House of Assembly passed legislation to incorporate it on May 8, 1754.

1749

Sephardic Jews in Charles Town organized Kahal Kadosh Beth Elohim, or Congregation Beth Elohim. This congregation was the place where ideas resembling Reform Judaism were first expressed in America.

1750

The estimated population of the colony, excluding Native Americans, was 65,000, of whom about two-thirds were enslaved Africans.

1751

MAY 17

Charles Town Huguenots established the South Carolina Society as a social and benevolent organization.

JUNE 14

The Parish of St. Philip's was divided; the part below Broad Street became the Parish of St. Michael's.

1752

SEPTEMBER 15 AND 30

Two great hurricanes hit Charles Town in succession.

1753

Construction of the State House commenced at the northwest corner of Broad and Meeting streets. It was occupied by 1756. At the same time construction of St. Michael's Church began on the southeast corner.

JULY 6

James Crokatt's announcement that he desired to retire as South Carolina's colonial agent resulted in a struggle between the Commons House and the Council over the selection of a successor. The Council lost both power and prestige in the contest.

1754

MAY 11

The Parish of St. Stephen was carved out of St. James Santee.

1755

More than 1,000 Acadians arrived from Nova Scotia. They did not assimilate, and by 1760 barely 200 remained in the province.

1756

The province purchased in London the ceremonial mace, which is still used by the legislature.

MAY 17

King George II declared war on France, thus formally began the Great War for the Empire (the French and Indian War, or Seven Years War). The declaration of war against France was proclaimed in Charles Town on September 2.

1757

MAY 21

Wealthy planters in the George Town area incorporated the Winyah Indigo Society as an agricultural and social club.

MAY 21

The Parish of St. Mark was carved out of Prince Frederick.

1759

NOVEMBER–DECEMBER

The beginnings of the Cherokee War in South Carolina. Gov. William Henry Lyttelton's expedition against the Cherokees ended after he took headmen Oconostota and Osteneco hostage and compelled them to agree to a hastily drawn treaty on December 22. The treaty did not keep the peace.

1760

The estimated population of the colony, excluding Native Americans, was 84,000, of whom about 52,000 were enslaved Africans.

JANUARY 12

The soldiers returning to Charles Town from the Cherokee campaign brought back smallpox and a virulent epidemic ensued.

MARCH 13

John Bartram, America's outstanding botanist, arrived at Charles Town to visit Dr. Alexander Garden and study southern plants during his first trip to South Carolina.

1761

FEBRUARY 1

Divine service was performed for the first time in St. Michael's Church.

MARCH 20

British troops from New York, accompanied by the South Carolina Provincial Regiment led by Thomas Middleton, marched under the command of Lt. Col. James Grant from Charles Town against the Cherokees. By July the Cherokees were defeated.

SEPTEMBER 23

Lt. Gov. William Bull negotiated a treaty with the Cherokees, the terms of which required the expulsion of all Frenchmen in Cherokee territory and the establishment of a dividing line that separated the Cherokees from South Carolina lands. By the end of the war the Cherokee population had been reduced to less than 7,000.

1762

JANUARY 12

John Stuart was appointed British Superintendent of Indian Affairs in the South. The commission, dated January 5, did not reach him until May 1762.

SEPTEMBER 13

Gov. Thomas Boone refused to administer the state oaths to Christopher Gadsden upon his election to the Commons House from St. Paul's Parish, a hotbed of dissent. This raised a constitutional crisis.

DECEMBER 16

The Commons House resolved to do no further business with the governor until he should recognize the rights and privileges of members of the Assembly. Little legislative business was transacted until after Boone left the province in May 1764.

1763

FEBRUARY 10

The Treaty of Paris ended the Great War for the Empire. It was proclaimed in Charles Town on August 27.

MAY

Gov. Boone and the Royal Council granted lands to Carolinians south of the Altamaha River in what is present-day Georgia.

NOVEMBER 10

The Treaty of Augusta was signed by the governors of Georgia, South Carolina, North Carolina, and Virginia, and by the chiefs of the Cherokees, Creeks, Chickasaws, Choctaws, and Catawbas. John Stuart as Superintendent of Indian Affairs for the Southern District presided over the conference. This treaty set aside a ten-square–mile reservation for the Catawbas.

1764

JULY 29

Packetboat service was established between Falmouth, England, and Charles Town, with the *Grenville Packet* arriving at Charles Town on this date.

III

Revolution
(1765–1790)

During the Great War for the Empire, Cherokee raids and continuous warfare destroyed the fragile social fabric of the South Carolina frontier. In 1766 and 1767, organized outlaw bands terrorized law-abiding backcountry settlers. When colonial authorities failed to respond to appeals for help, those who had a stake in society formed a vigilante movement and called themselves Regulators. After several years, with the assistance of authorities in Charlestown, order was restored.

By 1765 the English settlement originally called Charles Town had gotten into the habit of spelling its name as one word, Charlestown, and no doubt many of its citizens were already pronouncing it Charleston—although that did not become its official name until 1783, after the British were expelled.

No other colony had such close ties with England, for the great merchants of Charlestown owed much of their wealth to trade with, or through, London, a city they frequently visited. Thus, in their instincts, many South Carolinians were loyal to the British crown. By the misjudgment of George III's government in increasing taxes that might have slowed the colony's burgeoning economy, the insensitivity of the British governors in recognizing the needs and aspirations of the people (as in the case in 1772 of trying to move the capital from Charlestown to Beaufort), and perceived British threats to the bedrock of South Carolina's agricultural economy—its enslaved workers, brought South Carolina into the Revolution.

The Revolutionary War in South Carolina began and ended in Charlestown, but the conflict was won in the backcountry districts.

Partisan Bands led by Francis Marion (the "Swamp Fox"), Thomas Sumter (the "Gamecock"), and several others tied-up British resources in futile attempts to control the countryside. Then, in coordination with the Continental Army under Gen. Nathanael Greene, South Carolinians were able to liberate their state "by their own heroic courage and self-devotion, having suffered more, and dared more, and achieved more than the men of any other state."

After the war, Lowcountry South Carolina statesmen such as John Rutledge, Charles Cotesworth Pinckney, Charles Pinckney, Pierce Butler, and William Loughton Smith played major roles in the creation of the United States Constitution and the development of the new republic. During the 1780s the Lowcountry was forced to come to terms with the growing demands of backcountry residents (who by 1790 accounted for two-thirds of the white population of the state). Ædanus Burke, Wade Hampton, Andrew Pickens, Nathaniel Pendleton, and Robert Anderson were among the most prominent of the region's leaders. In cooperation with sympathetic Lowcountry legislators, they got the state capital moved from Charleston to Columbia and a new state constitution in 1790, which gave the backcountry greater representation and a share in state offices.

1765

MARCH 22

In England, Parliament passed the Stamp Act.

OCTOBER 7–25

John Rutledge, Christopher Gadsden, and Thomas Lynch represented South Carolina at the Stamp Act Congress, which was held in New York.

OCTOBER 18

The stamped paper arrived in Charlestown harbor.

OCTOBER 28

The stamp agents for South Carolina were coerced by a large crowd at Charlestown to promise not to issue any stamps until Parliament reviewed the act.

NOVEMBER 1

The Stamp Act went into effect. Clearances for ships could not be issued and courts could not conduct their business without stamped paper. The port was at a standstill.

NOVEMBER 29

The Commons House of Assembly, with only one dissenting vote, adopted the report of Gadsden's committee, which set forth the rights and duties of English subjects.

DECEMBER 25

There was threat of a slave insurrection.

1766

The St. Cecilia Society was organized in Charles Town as a private subscription concert organization.

JANUARY 1

On this date the slave trade was effectively cut off for a period of three years by the act which had been passed on August 5, 1764, to impose a £100 tax on each slave imported.

MARCH 18

Parliament repealed the Stamp Act and passed the Declaratory Act.

MAY 3

News of the repeal of the Stamp Act reached Charlestown. A great celebration was held that evening.

SEPTEMBER 12

The Reverend Charles Woodmason left Charlestown for the back-country where he became an advocate for the Regulators.

1767

Construction of the Exchange began in Charlestown at the east end of Broad Street under the direction of Peter and John Adam Horlbeck. It was completed in 1772.

MAY

Capt. James Hawker of HMS *Sardoine* seized the sloop *Active*. Thus began a major contest between the British authorities and the Carolina merchants.

MAY 23

The Parish of St. Luke was carved out of St. Helena's and the Parish of All Saints out of Prince George Winyah. Although these acts were disallowed and the new parishes dissolved in 1770, the Parish of All Saints was recreated on March 16, 1778, and the Parish of St. Luke on February 29, 1788.

OCTOBER 6

The governor issued a proclamation ordering those who led the Regulator movement in the backcountry to cease and desist.

NOVEMBER 7

The Regulators made a statement of their grievances.

1768

APRIL 12

The governor signed the Circuit Court Act which was designed to meet the grievances of the backcountry men who desired courts and jails. This law was disallowed in England because the royal government insisted that the judges should sit at the pleasure of the Crown.

The Parish of St. Matthew was established in Berkeley County and that of St. David in Craven County.

JUNE

The Regulators, at a meeting at the Congarees, adopted a Plan of Regulation to discipline "the baser sort of people."

JULY 25

There was a skirmish between the Regulators and the Provincial authorities at Mars Bluff on the Pee Dee River.

AUGUST 3

The governor issued a proclamation calling for the suppression of the Regulator movement.

AUGUST 6.

The governor by proclamation offered pardon to the Regulators who would drop their opposition to constituted authority.

OCTOBER 4–5

At this crucial election the power of the backcountry was first felt when many voters came down from the interior to vote at the parish churches.

NOVEMBER 19

Twenty-six members of the General Assembly voted unanimously to consider the Massachusetts Circular Letter and thereby brought on the dissolution of the Assembly by the royal governor. "Twenty-six" became a sacred number in Carolina's Revolutionary iconography. Armed opposition to the Regulators resulted in the formation of the Moderators—another vigilante group.

1769

MARCH 25

The Regulators and the Moderators negotiated a truce which brought the Regulation to an end.

JULY 22

A committee of thirteen merchants, thirteen planters, and thirteen mechanics convened to enforce the nonimportation agreements, which were South Carolina's protest against the Townshend duties passed by the English Parliament in 1767.

JULY 29

The General Assembly passed a second Circuit Court Act. The legislation created seven judicial districts—Charlestown was one district; Beaufort, Orangeburg, and Ninety Six made up the Southern circuit; Georgetown, Cheraw, and Camden comprised the Northern Circuit. British authorities let this law stand because the judges would now serve at the pleasure of the Crown. By the direction of this law, courts and jails were constructed in the six outlying districts by 1772.

DECEMBER 8

The General Assembly voted to send £1,500 sterling to support the cause of British radical John Wilkes in England.

1770

The estimated population of the province, excluding Native Americans, was 130,000; of that number, approximately 80,000 were enslaved Africans.

APRIL 14

When George III heard of South Carolina's gift to Wilkes, he ordered his government to send out an Additional Instruction, which denied the authority of the Assembly to appropriate funds for such a purpose and reaffirmed the coordinate authority of the Royal Council in the colony to amend and to pass money bills. An impasse thereupon ensued, which kept the Assembly from doing any real business for the remainder of the colonial period.

JULY 5

South Carolina raised its first public sculpture. The statue of William Pitt, designed by Joseph Wilton, which had been commissioned to honor South Carolina's English friend after the repeal of the Stamp Act, was erected in the crossing of Broad and Meeting streets.

DECEMBER 13

South Carolina broke through the nonimportation agreements, thereby opening up the port of Charlestown to commerce once again.

1771

MARCH 20

The General Assembly established an inspection system for tobacco at public warehouses on the principal rivers and at the ports. This was a sign that the backcountry had been filling up and had found a commercial crop.

OCTOBER 31

Gov. Charles Montague issues the Regulators full pardons.

1772

OCTOBER 8–10

Gov. Montagu called the Assembly to meet in Beaufort hoping thereby to control that body once it was removed from the influence of the Charlestown Patriots. This action would be referenced in the long list of indictments by the Patriots regarding the Crown in the Declaration of Independence: "He has called together legislative bodies at places unusual, uncomfortable, and distant from the depository of their public Records, for the sole purpose of fatiguing them into compliance with his measures."

NOVEMBER

The backcountry courts began to function. The judges held court on November 5 at Camden and Orangeburg, on November 16 at Cheraw and Ninety Six, on November 25 at Georgetown, and on November 30 at Beaufort.

1773

William Wofford established the first iron works in South Carolina at Lawson's Fork of the Pacolet River.

JANUARY

A committee of the Charlestown Library Society met to consider establishing a museum. This was the origin of the Charlestown Museum. In June Lt. Gov. William Bull II, president of the Library Society, announced the formation of a special committee for collecting materials.

MAY 10

The Tea Act became law.

DECEMBER 9

The Charlestown Chamber of Commerce was organized.

DECEMBER 22

The tea that had been brought to Charlestown under the Tea Act was unloaded and stored in the basement of the recently built Exchange.

1774

JULY 6–8

A General Meeting of the people in Charlestown elected Christopher Gadsden, Thomas Lynch, Henry Middleton, Edward Rutledge, and John Rutledge the province's delegates to the First Continental Congress. This meeting also selected a General Committee, headed by Charles Pinckney, to direct the interests of South Carolina during the turmoil.

OCTOBER 22–26

Henry Middleton served as the second president of the Continental Congress.

DECEMBER 1

On this date the continental nonimportation agreement went into effect.

1775

JANUARY 11–17

The first session of the First Provincial Congress met in Charlestown and selected Charles Pinckney president. The backcountry had 46 representatives in this extralegal legislative body of 184 delegates.

APRIL 21

Three days after Gen. Thomas Gage sent soldiers to Concord, Massachusetts to seize its gunpowder, Patriots in Charlestown moved to seize the public powder and arms in the magazines at Hobcaw, on Charlestown Neck, and at the State House.

MAY

A letter from Arthur Lee in London to Henry Laurens conveyed a rumor that the British intended to incite both enslaved people and Native Americans against the Patriots. This sensational rumor increased opposition to the royal government.

MAY 8

The news of the fighting at Lexington and Concord reached Charlestown.

JUNE 1–22

The second session of the First Provincial Congress met and selected Henry Laurens president.

JUNE 3

The members of the Provincial Congress voted unanimously to adopt the Continental Association to implement a boycott of British goods and an agreement not to export colonial products to Great Britain. They pledged to unite themselves in the defense of their state.

JUNE 14

The Provincial Congress by its own authority ordered the printing of £1 million currency.

JUNE 14

The Provincial Congress elected a Council of Safety with Henry Laurens selected president of the body.

JUNE 18

The last of the royal governors, Lord William Campbell, arrived in Charlestown.

JULY 12

South Carolina Patriots captured Fort Charlotte on the Savannah River.

AUGUST 18

Patriots in Charlestown hanged then burned the free Black pilot Thomas "Jerry" Jeremiah. Jeremiah was accused of instigating an insurrection and threatening to assist the Royal Navy when they came to punish the wayward Carolinians.

AUGUST–SEPTEMBER

William Henry Drayton, the Reverend Oliver Hart, and the Reverend William Tennent toured the backcountry to explain the Patriot position.

SEPTEMBER 10

On this date the continental nonexportation agreement went into effect. Rice, however, had been excepted from that agreement.

SEPTEMBER 15

Royal Gov. Lord William Campbell fled from his home on Meeting Street to HMS *Tamar* anchored in Charlestown harbor. He took with him the Great Seal of the Royal Province.

NOVEMBER 1–29

The first session of the Second Provincial Congress met and selected William Henry Drayton president.

NOVEMBER 11–12

In the first South Carolina engagement of the Revolution, HMS *Tamar* and HMS *Cherokee* fired upon the schooner *Defence* which was trying to sink four hulks to block Hog Island channel.

NOVEMBER 19–21

Tories attacked Major Andrew Williamson at Ninety Six. In this second engagement of the Revolution in South Carolina the first blood was shed.

DECEMBER

Col. Richard Richardson came to the aid of Williamson and pacified the backcountry. Because of the weather this became known as the Snow Campaign.

1776

FEBRUARY 1–MARCH 26

The second session of the Second Provincial Congress met.

FEBRUARY 8

Christopher Gadsden returned from Philadelphia carrying the first copies of Thomas Paine's *Common Sense* to South Carolina.

MARCH 26

South Carolina adopted its first state constitution which had been drawn up by the Provincial Congress. John Rutledge was elected the first president and Henry Laurens the first vice president.

APRIL 2

President Rutledge was authorized to design a Great Seal for the state.

APRIL 23

Chief Justice William Henry Drayton delivered an eloquent and inflammatory charge to the Charlestown grand jury upon the opening of South Carolina courts under the new constitution.

JUNE 1

British troops 2,500 strong landed on Long Island (Isle of Palms).

JUNE 28

At the Battle of Fort Moultrie, William Moultrie's band of Patriots, in their newly constructed palmetto log fort, repulsed the attempt of Sir Peter Parker to sail the British fleet into Charlestown harbor (the palmetto tree later became a state symbol). In the midst of the bombardment of Fort Moultrie Sergeant William Jasper rescued the flag. William Thompson's upcountrymen prevented Sir Henry Clinton's troops from crossing Breach Inlet from Long Island to Sullivan's Island.

JULY 2

The South Carolina delegation to the Continental Congress voted in favor of American Independence.

JULY 15–OCTOBER 11

Brig. Gen. Andrew Williamson directed the Cherokee Campaign in the Carolinas, crushing the Cherokee and compelling them to cede more than a million acres.

AUGUST 2

Arthur Middleton, Edward Rutledge, Thomas Lynch Jr., and Thomas Heyward Jr. signed the Declaration of Independence in Philadelphia.

AUGUST 5

The news of the adoption of the Declaration of Independence reached Charlestown.

1777

JANUARY 23

William Henry Drayton, at the direction of the South Carolina Assembly, presented a plan to the Georgia Convention under which South Carolina would annex its less populous neighbor. Georgia rejected the proposal the following day.

FEBRUARY 13

The General Assembly demanded of each white male citizen an oath of abjuration of loyalty to King George III and of allegiance to the new state. Those who would not take such an oath were banished.

MAY 20

By the Treaty of DeWitt's Corner between the Patriots and the Cherokees, South Carolina obtained most of present-day Greenville, Pickens, Oconee, and Anderson counties. Settlers immediately flocked to this backcountry area.

MAY 22

The state seal, which had been authorized on April 2, 1776, was used for the first time by President John Rutledge.

JUNE 13

The Marquis de Lafayette and the Baron de Kalb stepped ashore on North Island and made their way to the home of Benjamin Huger, having come from France to join the American cause.

JUNE 28

South Carolinians observed the first Palmetto Day in celebration of the Patriot victory at the Battle of Fort Moultrie.

NOVEMBER 1

Henry Laurens was elected president of the Continental Congress. He served until December 9, 1778.

1778

JANUARY 15

A great Charlestown fire destroyed, among other things, the library and the museum.

MARCH 6

Rawlins Lowndes was elected president of the state upon the resignation of John Rutledge, who could not accept the new constitution.

MARCH 7

The Continental frigate *Randolph* and four vessels of the South Carolina Navy fought an engagement with *HMS Yarmouth* east of Barbados. The *Randolph* exploded and the South Carolina Navy was dispersed.

MARCH 11

The General Assembly appointed Alexander Gillon, an ambitious Dutch merchant who had settled in Charlestown, Commodore of the South Carolina Navy.

MARCH 16

Orange Parish was cut off from St. Matthew's.

MARCH 19

South Carolina adopted its second state constitution, which disestablished the Church of England.

MARCH 28

A law passed under the new constitution demanded an assurance of fidelity to the state.

JULY 9

Henry Laurens, William Henry Drayton, John Mathews, Richard Hutson, and Thomas Heyward Jr. signed the Articles of Confederation, thereby signifying South Carolina's acceptance of that document.

NOVEMBER

The Southern campaign against Georgia and the Carolinas began with the arrival on the Georgia coast of Lt. Col. Archibald Campbell with British troops from the north.

1779

JANUARY 9

John Rutledge was elected the state's first governor.

FEBRUARY 3

The British attempted an amphibious landing at Port Royal Island but were driven off by Continental troops commanded by Gen. William Moultrie and South Carolina militia led by Brigadier Gen. Stephen Bull.

FEBRUARY 14

At the Battle of Kettle Creek in Georgia Andrew Pickens defeated a larger Loyalist force from North Carolina.

JUNE 20

Gen. William Moultrie attacked Augustine Prevost who had retreated from the walls of Charlestown to the ferry at Stono River.

OCTOBER 9

A major assault on the defenses of Savannah failed to carry the city. Sergeant William Jasper and the Comte Casimir Pulaski died in the attack.

1780

The estimated population of the state was 180,000, of whom about 97,000 were enslaved Africans.

FEBRUARY 3

Facing a British offensive, the General Assembly vested extraordinary emergency powers in Gov. John Rutledge for a period to end ten days after the next meeting of the legislature. Thus the governor became "Dictator" Rutledge.

FEBRUARY 11

Sir Henry Clinton disembarked his army on Johns Island.

MARCH 27

Two great cavalry leaders, Col. Banastre Tarleton and Col. William Washington, clashed near Rantowle's Bridge over the Stono River.

MARCH 29

The British began a siege of Charlestown, Clinton by land, the ships of Marriot Arbuthnot by sea.

APRIL 14

Tarleton and Major Patrick Ferguson dispersed the Patriot forces commanded by Gen. Isaac Huger at Moncks Corner and thereby cut off the escape route from Charlestown for Benjamin Lincoln's forces.

MAY 6

Fort Moultrie fell to the British.

MAY 9–12

The bombardment of Charlestown.

MAY 12

Gen. Lincoln surrendered Charlestown, with over 5,000 troops and 50,000 pounds of gunpower, to Gen. Clinton.

MAY 29

Tarleton caught the fleeing Abraham Buford and his Virginians at the Waxhaws and cut them down.

MAY 30

Commodore Gillon and the Chevalier de Luxembourg signed a contract in France in which the frigate *Indien* was turned over to Gillon for a term of three years. Gillon renamed the *Indien* the *South Carolina.*

JUNE 3

Clinton abrogated the terms of surrender, revoking paroles and demanding South Carolinians take an oath of allegiance to the King.

JUNE 5

The loyal citizens of Charlestown presented addresses of congratulation to Clinton and Arbuthnot. Those who signed had their estates confiscated by the Patriot legislature when it met at Jacksonborough in January-February 1782.

JUNE 8

Clinton sailed for New York leaving Gen. Charles Lord Cornwallis in command at Charlestown.

JUNE 18

Loyalist Christian Huck destroyed William Hill's Iron Works in the New Acquisition District.

JULY 12

Huck was killed and his Loyalist force defeated at Williamson's Plantation in a bloody action, typical of the fighting in the South Carolina backcountry. Six other partisan victories followed so that by the end of the month, the Patriots had gotten the upper hand in Spartan and New Acquisition districts.

AUGUST 6

Thomas Sumter, trying to organize resistance in the backcountry, attacked the Loyalists at Hanging Rock.

AUGUST 15, 16

Gen. Charles Lord Cornwallis defeated Horatio Gates at the Battle of Camden, where Baron de Kalb lost his life.

AUGUST 18

Tarleton surprised Sumter at Fishing Creek.

AUGUST 27

On this evening the British took into custody twenty-nine prominent Charlestonians including Christopher Gadsden. They and
others were later shipped off to St. Augustine.

SEPTEMBER 19

The loyal citizens of Charlestown presented Cornwallis with an
address of congratulations for his victory at Camden. Those who
participated had their estates confiscated by the Patriot legislature
when it met at Jacksonborough in January–February 1782.

SEPTEMBER 29

Francis Marion struck at the loyal militia led by John Coming Ball
at Black Mingo Creek Bridge.

OCTOBER 6

Henry Laurens was imprisoned in the Tower of London. On September 3, while on a mission from Congress to Holland to seek a
loan, he had been taken on the high seas of Newfoundland and sent
to London. He remained in the Tower until December 31, 1781, at
which time he was exchanged for Lord Cornwallis.

OCTOBER 7

Patriot militia from South Carolina, North Carolina, Virginia,
Georgia, and the over-the-mountain men defeated the Loyalist militia raised by Major Patrick Ferguson at the Battle of King's Mountain, one of the decisive battles of the Revolution.

NOVEMBER 9

Sumter repulsed the British cavalry at Fishdam Ford and barely
escaped a small party the British sent to kill him.

NOVEMBER 20

At Blackstock's plantation in a bend of the Tyger River, Sumter
fought Tarleton to a standoff.

DECEMBER 2

Gen. Nathanael Greene arrived at Charlotte, North Carolina, to
take command of the Southern Continental Army.

1781

JANUARY 17

Daniel Morgan defeated Tarleton at the Battle of Cowpens. This
was the first battle of the Revolution where British regulars fled
the field in the face of an American army. Morgan's battle plan of

defense in depth is still studied by military officers in this country and abroad. Many military historians consider it to be the crucial battle of the American Revolution.

JANUARY 25

Francis Marion with the assistance of Light Horse Harry Lee captured the British commander at Georgetown.

FEBRUARY 14

Greene crossed the Dan River to safety in Virginia after leading Cornwallis in a chase through North Carolina.

MARCH 15

Greene faced Cornwallis at the Battle of Guilford Courthouse. The battle was a draw, but Cornwallis soon marched his depleted army north to Yorktown.

APRIL 23

Lee and Marion, again cooperating, forced the surrender of Fort Watson on the Santee River after Hezekiah Maham built a wooden tower which permitted the Patriots to rake the interior of the fort with gunfire.

APRIL 25

Col. Francis Lord Rawdon defeated Greene at Hobkirk's Hill just north of Camden.

MAY 8–12

The siege of Fort Motte concluded when Rebecca Motte urged the Patriots to shoot flaming arrows into her home, which the British were using as a fort.

MAY 11

Orangeburg surrendered to Sumter.

MAY 15

Fort Granby on the Congaree surrendered to Lee.

MAY 22-JUNE 19

Nathanael Greene besieged Ninety Six, the last of the British garrisons in the upcountry, until Lord Rawdon raised the siege after he had received reinforcements in Charlestown.

AUGUST 4

The British executed Isaac Hayne in Charlestown.

SEPTEMBER 8

The Battle of Eutaw Springs, the bloodiest encounter in the Southern Campaign, was the last major engagement in the state.

NOVEMBER 8

After retiring to the High Hills of the Santee after the Battle of Eutaw Springs, Greene once again invaded the Lowcountry and established his army at Round O in Colleton County.

DECEMBER

The British abandoned Dorchester, their post on the Ashley River, which has remained a ruin ever since.

1782

JANUARY 8–FEBRUARY 26

The South Carolina General Assembly under the protection of Greene's army met at Jacksonborough on the Edisto River to restore civil government to the state.

JANUARY 31

John Mathews was elected governor after Gadsden refused the honor.

FEBRUARY 26

The estates of many Loyalists were confiscated.

FEBRUARY 26

South Carolina ratified an amendment to the Articles of Confederation which would have permitted the Continental Congress to levy a 5 percent ad valorem import duty.

AUGUST 27

John Laurens was killed at Combahee Bluff, in one of the last minor engagements of the Revolution, by a British force in search of supplies for the besieged garrison of Charlestown.

SEPTEMBER 6

A British fleet sailed into Charlestown harbor to evacuate the British force stationed there.

NOVEMBER 14

Dills Bluff (James Island) was the last Revolutionary battle in the state.

NOVEMBER 30

In Paris, Henry Laurens, along with Benjamin Franklin, John Adams, and John Jay, signed the preliminary treaty of peace.

DECEMBER 14

British forces evacuated Charlestown, taking away some 4,200 Loyalists and 5,000 enslaved Africans.

1783

By this year Gideon DuPont had perfected the tidal culture of rice. It is impossible to pin to one date such a fundamental change in the cultivation of rice, the state's leading staple. Yet by the 1780s rice was being grown in the river swamps where the fluctuation of the tides could be used to flood and drain the fields.

AUGUST 13

The General Assembly passed legislation incorporating Charleston as a city in a move designed to restore order to a community still wracked by turbulence. The name of the city was henceforth "Charleston."

AUGUST 29

Gen. William Moultrie called the Continental officers to meet at the City Tavern, northeast corner of Church and Broad streets, to form the South Carolina chapter of the Society of the Cincinnati.

SEPTEMBER 23

The Peace of Paris ended the war of the American Revolution. Despite the state's tremendous losses during the war, South Carolina was the only state to meet its financial obligations to Congress this year.

1784

MARCH 26

The Alien Act of 1784 expressly defined the manner in which an alien could become a citizen of the new state.

1785

Ann Donovan Timothy began to publish the *State Gazette of South-Carolina* and became "Printer to the State."

MARCH 19

The General Assembly passed legislation that incorporated the College of Charleston. Students were accepted by 1790. An attempt to establish colleges at Winnsborough and Ninety Six at this time failed.

MARCH 24

The County Court Act divided the state into counties and established a system of county courts. These courts were abolished in

1799. Abbeville, Laurens, Spartanburg, Newberry, Union, York, Chester, Fairfield, Lewisburg (Lexington), Richland, Lancaster, Chesterfield, Darlington, Marlboro, Barnwell, Williamsburg, and Winton (Edgefield) were included in the act.

AUGUST 24

A group of Lowcountry planters formed the South Carolina Society for Promoting and Improving Agriculture and Other Rural Concerns in order to search for new staple alternatives to rice and indigo.

OCTOBER 12

The General Assembly authorized an issue of £100,000 in paper bills in order to spark the new economy.

1786

MARCH 11

South Carolina ratified an amendment to the Articles of Confederation which would have given the Continental Congress the power to regulate commerce with foreign nations. Having ratified the amendment, South Carolina saw no reason to send a delegation to the Annapolis convention.

MARCH 13

Charles Pinckney, a delegate to the Continental Congress, urged the legislature of New Jersey to contribute its assessment to support the government of the Confederation. In this speech Pinckney outlined needed changes in the central government, the seed of the Pinckney plan of 1787.

MARCH 22

The General Assembly created Greenville County from land acquired from the Cherokees during the American Revolution. The General Assembly passed legislation which incorporated the Santee Canal Company. A canal which linked the Santee and Cooper rivers was opened by 1799.

The General Assembly agreed to move the capital of the state to the upcountry. The new town would be called Columbia and would be situated near Friday's Ferry on the Congaree River on land two miles square, including the plain of the hill owned by Thomas and James Taylor.

MAY 3

Charles Pinckney inaugurated an ambitious movement in the Congress to reorganize the government under the Articles of Confederation.

SEPTEMBER 29

Scottish merchants in Charleston organized the South Carolina Golf Club. Until 1800 the game of golf was played on Harleston's Green in Charleston.

1787

Jonathan Lucas built the first tidal rice mill at John Bowman's Peach Island plantation on the Santee River. John Gabriel Guignard laid out Columbia.

MARCH 28

The General Assembly prohibited the foreign slave trade for a period of three years. As this legislation was several times renewed, the slave trade was cut off until 1803.

MAY 29

Charles Pinckney presented his plan to the Constitutional Convention in Philadelphia.

SEPTEMBER 17

John Rutledge, Charles Cotesworth Pinckney, Charles Pinckney, and Pierce Butler signed the new Constitution of the United States.

1788

JANUARY 19

The General Assembly agreed to call a convention of the people to consider the ratification of the Constitution.

FEBRUARY 5

The State House in Charleston burned. Construction of the new State House in Columbia had already begun.

MAY 12–23

The Constitutional Ratification Convention met in Charleston. South Carolina ratified the document May 23.

NOVEMBER 4

The General Assembly passed a law which permitted the payment of certain debts in five installments. This type of law was void under the new US Constitution, which forbade the states from impairing the obligation of contracts.

George Washington was elected President. South Carolina cast seven electoral votes for him, six for John Rutledge, and one for John Hancock.

1789

David Ramsay published in two volumes *The History of the American Revolution.*

DECEMBER 1

The records of the state were moved from Charleston to Columbia.

1790

US Census

White	140,178
Enslaved African American	107,094
Free African American	1,801
Total	249,073

William Elliott first planted Sea Island cotton at the northwest point of Hilton Head Island.

JANUARY 4

The first session of the General Assembly to be held in Columbia opened.

JANUARY 18–19

South Carolina ratified the Bill of Rights (the first ten amendments of the US Constitution).

MAY 10–JUNE 3

A state constitutional convention met in Columbia to write the third state constitution. The first two constitutions had been written by the legislative branch. The third state constitution was not sent out to the people for ratification.

NOVEMBER 1

Free African American and racially mixed men in Charleston founded the Brown Fellowship Society as a benevolent society.

South Carolina and the Union
(1791–1859)

Except for the War of 1812 with Great Britain, South Carolina and the other states of the Union were isolated from such upheavals in Europe as the French Revolution (1789–1799). South Carolina shared the troubles, especially the fiscal troubles, of the young nation, but recovered a great deal of its prosperity as cotton exports boomed after 1800. While the industrial revolution was taking place in the Northern states, South Carolina, despite the presence of inventors and innovators (like Abraham Blanding, Robert Mills, and later James M. Legare), talent for management that the planters had long since developed, and obvious opportunities for water-powered mills (a few of which were indeed started), remained a staple-exporting region, importing manufactured goods from England and the North. In this, and in the slave trade that reopened until 1808 and at times even illegally until the middle of the nineteenth century, lay South Carolina's tragedy. Outside the Southern states, the civilized world came more and more to see slavery as an ugly anachronism. Proposals from the Northern manufacturing states to levy tariffs on manufactured imports jeopardized South Carolina's economic system and were deftly resisted by John C. Calhoun, who developed the first critique of the rapidly centralizing forces in the United States and the spiritual bankruptcy of industrial civilization.

In the 1820s many whites moved southwest to Alabama, Mississippi, Louisiana, and Texas, taking with them the system of exporting slave-cultivated cotton while adding sugar to the staple crops. South Carolina was at first in a lonely position, for no other Southern state owed so much wealth to enslaved labor. But gradually the skillful diplomacy of South Carolina's leaders, the emigration that resulted in like-minded communities in the west, the eagerness of industrialists in the middle Atlantic states to penalize foreign competitors with tariffs, and the steadily growing abhorrence of slavery among those who did not own enslaved people or feel indebted to slave owners, led to a coalition of Southern states behind the intellectual leadership of South Carolina.

It must be remembered, however, that a great many white South Carolinians never owned slaves, that a very small minority of them opposed the perpetuation of slavery and moved north of the Ohio River, and that many opposed separation from the Union and from the modern way of life that it was coming to embody. Nevertheless, a Southern style of life that included fear as well as exploitation of the enslaved African Americans united most white South Carolinians in defense of slavery.

It was wisdom, not cowardice, that prevented most African Americans in South Carolina from openly rising in rebellion, for if a slave rebellion failed it would only harden the determination of the whites and if it succeeded where could the self-emancipators settle safely, prosperously, and in large numbers? Resistance was unceasing, however, although most often it took the form of smaller acts of insubordination or was articulated through cultural defiance.

During the period from American independence to the Civil War, many white South Carolinians enjoyed enough freedom and ease to allow the arts, especially architecture, to flourish. South Carolina College rapidly became an intellectual center that flourished unlike any college in the South had before, and like hardly any have since. But perhaps the most positive achievement of the age was the development of a characteristically Southern celebration of rural and agricultural values by such writers as William Grayson and William Gilmore Simms.

1791

The revolt of the enslaved people in Santo Domingo raised the specter of a slave rebellion in America. Many French Catholics fleeing the chaos of that island found a haven in Charleston.

JANUARY 3

The new state constitution went into effect.

FEBRUARY 19

The General Assembly created Kershaw County.

The General Assembly incorporated the Jewish Congregation of Beth Elohim in Charleston under article 8, section 1 of the new state constitution which granted the free exercise of religion. That same day, the Assembly incorporated the congregation of St. Mary's as the Roman Catholic Church of Charleston.

APRIL 27–MAY 28

President George Washington entered the state at Little River and proceeded to Georgetown, Charleston, and Savannah before returning to the north by Augusta and Columbia.

1792

In the case *Bowman v. Middleton,* a South Carolina court first declared a state law unconstitutional.

MARCH 9

Stockholders of the First Bank of the United States opened a branch in Charleston.

NOVEMBER 2–DECEMBER 5

George Washington was reelected. South Carolina cast eight electoral votes for him, seven for John Adams, and one for Aaron Burr.

1793

In this year, the first sizable cotton shipments were made from Charleston. The recent invention of the roller gin by Abraham Eve for Sea Island cotton and the saw-toothed gin by Eli Whitney for upland cotton made the increase in production possible.

APRIL

Edmond-Charles Genêt ("Citizen Genet") arrived in Charleston on his way to Philadelphia to present his credentials as envoy of the new French republic.

1794

Engineers begin plans for Castle Pinckney that was to be built on Shute's Folly in Charleston. Construction began in 1797; work was completed by 1809 when it was considered the strongest fortification in the harbor.

FEBRUARY

Charleston Mechanic Society, founded with 74 members, became the state's first labor organization. The members of the society contributed their labor for the erection of Fort Mechanic on High Battery.

MAY 10

The General Assembly passed legislation incorporating the Medical Society of South Carolina.

1795

SEPTEMBER 13

The Reverend Robert Smith was consecrated the first Episcopal Bishop of South Carolina at Christ Church in Philadelphia.

DECEMBER 15

The United States Senate rejected the nomination of John Rutledge to be Chief Justice of the United States Supreme Court.

1796

JUNE 13

Another great Charleston fire devastated the city and consumed many of the houses and public buildings between Bay and Church streets, north from Broad Street to St. Philip's Church.

NOVEMBER 4–DECEMBER 7

John Adams was elected president. South Carolina cast eight electoral votes for Thomas Jefferson and eight for Thomas Pinckney. Jefferson edged out Pinckney for the vice presidency of the United States.

1797

OCTOBER 27

The XYZ Affair. When one of the French negotiators asked for a "douceur," Charles Cotesworth Pinckney replied: "No, no, not a sixpence." Robert Goodloe Harper coined the phrase "Millions for Defense But Not One Cent for Tribute" as a toast at a banquet in Philadelphia given in John Marshall's honor, June 18, 1798.

DECEMBER 16

The General Assembly passed legislation incorporating the Mutual Insurance Company and the Charleston Insurance Company, one for fire and the other for marine insurance, as the first insurance companies incorporated by the state.

1798

MAY 5

Charlestonians held a mass meeting in St. Michael's Church to consider the threat of an invasion from the French West Indies.

JULY 19

Gov. Charles Pinckney called the legislators to meet at his home on Meeting Street in Charleston to put the state in a posture of defense.

DECEMBER 21

The General Assembly created Barnwell, Sumter, and Colleton counties.

1799

FEBRUARY 8

A great celebration in Charleston for the return of Charles Cotesworth Pinckney from France after the "XYZ Affair" culminated in a banquet at City Hall in the Exchange.

JUNE 5

The sloop of war *John Adams*, built by Paul Pritchard in Charleston and funded by public subscription was launched. The vessel was one of the oldest vessels in the US Navy at the time of its decommissioning in 1867.

DECEMBER 18

Commissioners began to lay out streets on Sullivan's Island, which had become a summer resort during the 1790s.

DECEMBER 21

The General Assembly chartered Charleston's first public utility, the Charleston Water Company, to bring Goose Creek water to Charleston.

1800

US Census

White	196,255
Enslaved African American	146,151
Free African American	3,185
Total	345,591

JANUARY 1

The General Assembly passed legislation that reorganized the entire system of courts within the state.

OCTOBER 31–DECEMBER 3

Thomas Jefferson was elected president. South Carolina cast eight electoral votes for him and eight for Aaron Burr.

DECEMBER 20

The General Assembly passed legislation which made it more difficult to emancipate. Until 1800 an enslaved person could be manumitted by will or deed. After that year freeholders of the neighborhood had to certify that the freed person could support his or her family.

1801

The General Assembly created Horry District out of Georgetown Judicial District.

MARCH 17

Irish immigrants organized the Hibernian Society as a social and charitable organization to provide aid to immigrants and their families.

DECEMBER 19

The General Assembly passed legislation which chartered two state banks, the Bank of South Carolina and the State Bank.

The state appropriated $50,000 to pay Phineas Miller and Eli Whitney for the right of South Carolina planters to use their machine called "a saw gin, for cleaning the staple of cotton from the seed." After some difficulties the inventors collected.

In order to promote greater unity, the legislature chartered the South Carolina College to be placed at the center of the state. After the Civil War it became the University of South Carolina.

1803

Workers laid the cornerstone of Mount Dearborn Armory, which was originally intended to become one of three Federal Arsenals, near Rocky Mount.

JANUARY 10

The *Charleston Courier* began publication. This paper is still published as the *Post and Courier*.

DECEMBER 17

The General Assembly reopened the foreign slave trade. More than 40,000 enslaved people would be imported during the next five years before the federal ban went into effect January 1, 1808.

1804

Moses Waddel opened Willington Academy, a prestigious classical school for boys.

MAY 7

William Johnson was sworn in as an associate justice of the United States Supreme Court.

NOVEMBER 2–DECEMBER 5

Thomas Jefferson defeated Federalist Charles Cotesworth Pinckney for the presidency of the United States. South Carolina cast ten electoral votes for Jefferson.

DECEMBER 6

John Gaillard was elected to the US Senate, where he served until his death on February 26, 1826. He was elected president pro tempore on February 28, 1810, and on several later occasions.

1805

JANUARY 10

The College of South Carolina opened its doors in Columbia.

AUGUST 28

Christopher Gadsden, the former leader of the Sons of Liberty, died a Federalist.

1806

OCTOBER 28

A Charleston city ordinance restricted the movement of free African Americans.

1807

DECEMBER 22

The Embargo Act that banned all trade with foreign countries went into effect. The commercial life of Charleston never fully recovered from this cessation of foreign trade until after World War II.

1808

Many South Carolina Quakers moved to the Old Northwest in order to escape the institution of slavery.

JANUARY 1

The foreign slave trade came to an end by federal law at the earliest possible date under the US Constitution.

OCTOBER 24

Workers laid the cornerstone of the South Carolina Homespun Company at the west end of Wentworth Street in Charleston. The General Assembly passed legislation incorporating this, the first manufacturing company in the state, on December 15, 1808.

NOVEMBER 4–DECEMBER 7

James Madison defeated Federalist Charles Cotesworth Pinckney for the presidency of the United States. South Carolina cast ten electoral votes for Madison.

DECEMBER 17

An amendment to the state constitution, the result of the "Compromise of 1808," provided for more equal representation between the Upcountry and the Lowcountry. It also provided for reapportionment of the House of Representatives every ten years.

1809

DECEMBER

David Ramsay published the two volume *The History of South-Carolina from its first Settlement in 1670, to the Year 1808.*

1810

The third census of the United States showed that the institution of slavery had spread throughout the state.

White	214,196
Enslaved African American	196,365
Free African American	4,554
Total	415,115

DECEMBER 19

By an amendment to the state constitution "every white man of the age of twentyone years" could henceforth vote after a residence of six months.

1811

MARCH 11

The South Carolina War Hawks (who favored war with Great Britain), John C. Calhoun, William Lowndes, and David R. Williams, took their seats in Congress for the first time.

DECEMBER 21

The General Assembly passed legislation to appropriate funds for "Free Schools" throughout the state.

1812

JUNE 19

President Madison officially announced that the country was at war with Great Britain.

OCTOBER 30–DECEMBER 2

James Madison defeated DeWitt Clinton for reelection to the presidency. South Carolina cast eleven electoral votes for Madison.

DECEMBER 19

The General Assembly passed legislation which chartered the Bank of the State of South Carolina. Although there had been earlier state-chartered banks, this was the first state-owned bank.

1813

AUGUST 22

The British landed forces at Beaufort and on Hilton Head where marauders plundered settlements.

AUGUST 27–28

A great hurricane, surpassed only by those of 1752, 1893, and 1989, struck the South Carolina coast.

1814

JANUARY 19

Langdon Cheves won election as speaker of the United States House of Representatives succeeding Henry Clay.

1815

Upcountry planters organized the Pendleton Farmers' Society. The group advocated crop diversification and urged South Carolinians to remain in the state in the face of numerous migrations to the west. By 1860, about one-half of persons born in South Carolina lived in another Southern state.

1816

Philip Weaver, a master textile mechanic from Coventry, Rhode Island, began the South Carolina Cotton Manufactory in Spartanburg. By 1826 he had left the state because of financial difficulties and his opposition to slavery.

MARCH 22.

A treaty with the Cherokees, signed in Washington, DC, secured the westernmost tip of South Carolina from the Native Americans. The state approved on December 19, 1816, and by an amendment of the state constitution of December 20, 1820, this land became a part of Pendleton District.

JULY

Camden officials thwarted an abortive slave insurrection.

NOVEMBER 1–DECEMBER 4

James Monroe defeated Rufus King for the presidency. South Carolina cast eleven electoral votes for Monroe.

DECEMBER 4.

William Smith, the originator of the South Carolina states' rights position, won election to the US Senate where he held a seat until March 3, 1823.

1817

By 1817, the Landrum family were producing alkaline-glazed "Edgefield" pottery at Pottersville.

DECEMBER 8

John C. Calhoun took the oath of office as Secretary of War.

DECEMBER 17

The state appointed an engineer to superintend public buildings and civil and military works. In this, the state's largest internal improvement program got under way. In 1820 the state established a Board of Public Works which gave way in 1822 to a Superintendent of Public Works. This program of building roads, canals, and court houses came to a close in 1828 as the railroad emerged on the scene.

1818

JANUARY

The price of short-staple cotton in the Charleston market reached thirty-five cents per pound, the peak of cotton prices in the antebellum period.

1819

MAY 22

The steamship *Savannah* under the command of Capt. Moses Rogers departed Savannah for Liverpool. This was an attempt to reestablish direct trade with England from the southeastern ports.

DECEMBER 3

Thomas Cooper began his appointment as professor of Chemistry at South Carolina College. A year later he assumed the office of temporary president and in December 1821 won election as president of the College.

1820

US Census

White	237,440
Enslaved African American	258,475
Free African American	6,826
Total	502,741

FEBRUARY 14

Congressman Charles Pinckney stated that it was not the intention of those who met in Philadelphia in 1787 to have included persons of color in the meaning of the word "citizen" in the privileges and immunities clause of the US Constitution.

SEPTEMBER 21

John England was consecrated the first Roman Catholic Bishop of South Carolina in St. Finbar's Cathedral in Cork, Ireland. Bishop England landed in Charleston on December 30, 1820. He died April 11, 1842.

NOVEMBER 1 – DECEMBER 6

James Monroe won reelection to the presidency without a major opponent. South Carolina cast eleven electoral votes for him.

DECEMBER 20

Henceforth no enslaved person could be freed without the formal consent of the state legislature, nor could free persons of color enter the state.

1821

MAY 15

Sarah Grimké, the eldest daughter of John F. Grimké, sailed for Philadelphia thus making a statement in opposition to slavery. Her sister Angelina joined her in 1829, motivated by a similar animosity towards slavery. They became prominent abolitionists.

DECEMBER 20

The General Assembly passed legislation that incorporated the South Carolina Academy of Fine Arts.

DECEMBER 20

The General Assembly passed legislation that authorized the building of a lunatic asylum and a school for the deaf and dumb at or near Columbia. Designed by Robert Mills and embodying new ideas about the treatment of the mentally ill, the asylum received its first patient on December 12, 1828.

1822

Major Alexander Garden published his *Anecdotes of the Revolutionary War in America*.

JUNE – JULY

Fear of a slave insurrection swept Charleston.

JUNE 17

Following the betrayal of a specific plot and hasty investigation, authorities launched a search for conspirators and made the first of 131 arrests, including alleged ringleader Denmark Vesey, a free African American.

JUNE 28

A Court of Magistrates and Freeholders convicted Vesey of inciting an insurrection. He was hanged on July 2.

In response to the Vesey plot, Charleston officials ordered the African Methodist Episcopal Church Charleston to be closed. Reorganized in 1865 as Emanuel A.M.E. Church, it became a focal point for Black political activity.

SEPTEMBER 27–28

A tremendous hurricane struck the coast near Georgetown. It was worse than the Winyah hurricane of September 10–11, 1820. Many persons on North Island and in the Santee delta were washed away.

DECEMBER 21

The General Assembly passed legislation that established a municipal guard of 150 men for Charleston. The Arsenal and Guard House were to be established in the tobacco inspection warehouse as it was no longer needed since tobacco had declined as a backcountry staple.

DECEMBER 21

The General Assembly passed the first of the Negro Seamen's Acts. Any free African American coming into Charleston on a vessel would be lodged in the local jail during the stay of the vessel in port. If the captain would not pay the cost of board and lodging, the sailor could be sold into slavery.

1823

Construction began on Robert Mills' Fireproof Building in Charleston.

AUGUST 7

In a federal court decision in the case of *Elkison v. Deliesseline,* Judge William Johnson ruled that the recent Seamen's Act was in conflict with the commerce and treaty-making powers of the United States Constitution.

DECEMBER 20

The South Carolina General Assembly passed a second Seamen's Act.

DECEMBER 20

The General Assembly passed legislation requiring two copies of the Great Seal be made, one for the secretary of state's office in Charleston, the other for the secretary of state's office in Columbia, symbolic of the two centers of authority in the state.

1824

JANUARY

Workers completed the Columbia Canal

OCTOBER 26–DECEMBER 2

John Quincy Adams defeated Andrew Jackson, William Crawford, and Henry Clay for the presidency. South Carolina cast eleven electoral votes for Andrew Jackson.

NOVEMBER 21

Modern Reform Judaism was born when members of the Beth Elohim congregation in Charleston organized the Reformed Society of Israelites.

DECEMBER 17

The legislature created the state's first Court of Appeals. The new three-judge court sat alternately in Columbia and Charleston.

1825

MARCH

The Marquis de Lafayette made a triumphal tour through the state. He reached Fayetteville, North Carolina, on March 4, then proceeded to Cheraw, Camden, Columbia, and Charleston whence he sailed to Savannah on March 17.

MARCH

President Adams appointed Joel R. Poinsett minister to Mexico. A showy Mexican plant was named poinsettia in his honor.

MARCH 4

John C. Calhoun took the oath of office of vice president of the United States.

DECEMBER 15–16

The House and Senate of South Carolina adopted resolutions protesting against a broad interpretation of the taxing and spending powers of the federal government.

1826

DECEMBER 20

The General Assembly divided Pendleton District into Anderson and Pickens Districts.

DECEMBER 20

The General Assembly passed legislation which incorporated the first South Carolina Bar Association.

1827

FEBRUARY–MARCH

Robert Y. Hayne spoke out in the United States Senate against federal appropriations for the American Colonization Society.

JULY 2

Thomas Cooper, president of South Carolina College, delivered a speech in Columbia in which he questioned the political relationship between the North and South.

NOVEMBER 18

Eighteen-year-old Edgar Allan Poe began thirteen months' garrison duty at Fort Moultrie on Sullivan's Island. During this period he gathered material for his story "The Gold Bug."

DECEMBER 19

The General Assembly passed legislation that chartered the South Carolina Canal and Rail Road Company.

1828

FEBRUARY

The Southern Review began publication in Charleston. It continued until 1832.

OCTOBER 31–DECEMBER 2

Andrew Jackson defeated John Quincy Adams for the presidency. John C. Calhoun was elected Vice President on the same ticket. South Carolina cast eleven electoral votes for them.

DECEMBER 19

The legislature endorsed the *Exposition and Protest* (secretly written by Vice President Calhoun) that argued the unconstitutionality of the protective tariff.

1829

The lower portion of "The State Road" that eventually linked Columbia and Charleston was completed.

Daniel A. Payne, an eighteen-year-old free African American, opened a school for Black children in a house on Tradd Street in Charleston.

Construction began on Fort Sumter on a man-made island in Charleston harbor.

The Reverend William Capers began his Methodist mission to the enslaved.

JULY 23

An abortive slave insurrection was discovered and thwarted in Georgetown County.

1830

US Census

White	257,863
Enslaved African American	315,401
Free African American	7,921
Total	581,185

JANUARY 19–27

The famous debate between Senator Robert Y. Hayne and Senator Daniel Webster on the topics of western land, protectionist tariffs, and the nature of the United States Constitution took place in Washington, DC.

APRIL 13

At a Thomas Jefferson birthday celebration in Washington, DC, President Andrew Jackson toasted: "Our Federal Union—It must be preserved." Vice President John C. Calhoun replied: "The Union—Next to our liberties the most dear."

1831

JULY 26

John C. Calhoun wrote a letter to the *Pendleton Messenger* openly avowing his nullification philosophy.

SEPTEMBER

The price of short staple cotton in the Charleston market reached the bottom price of nine cents per pound.

OCTOBER

John James Audubon and John Bachman met in Charleston. Their friendship nurtured a closer study of nature. Two Audubon sons married Bachman daughters.

DECEMBER 17

The General Assembly passed legislation which chartered the Medical College of the State of South Carolina. It opened in 1833.

1832

AUGUST 11

Caroline Gilman began editing *The Rose Bud, or Youth's Gazette,* the first children's paper in the country.

JULY 14

Congress passed the Tariff of 1832 which helped to set the nullification crisis in motion.

NOVEMBER 2–DECEMBER 5

Andrew Jackson defeated Henry Clay, John Floyd, and William Wirt to be reelected to the presidency. South Carolina cast eleven electoral votes for Nullifier Party candidate Floyd.

NOVEMBER 19–24

The Nullification Convention met in Columbia.

NOVEMBER 24

The Ordinance of Nullification nullified the Tariff Acts of 1828 and 1832. The Convention also adopted "An Address to the People of South Carolina" by Robert J. Turnbull and "An Address to the States of the Union" by John C. Calhoun and George McDuffie.

DECEMBER 10

Jackson issued a proclamation condemning treason in South Carolina.

DECEMBER 21

Gov. Robert Hayne, who had just succeeded James Hamilton, issued his own counter-proclamation.

DECEMBER 28

Calhoun resigned as Vice President of the United States.

1833

JANUARY 4

Calhoun resumed his seat in the United States Senate.

JANUARY 21

A convention assembled in Charleston to postpone the date on which the Ordinance of Nullification was to have gone into effect (February 1, 1833).

MARCH 2

Congress passed and the President signed the Tariff of 1833 and the Force Bill into law.

MARCH 15

South Carolina repealed the Ordinance of Nullification and on March 18 nullified the Force Act.

OCTOBER

Workers completed the steam railroad from Charleston to Hamburg, a distance of 136 miles. At the time it was the longest railroad in the world.

DECEMBER 19

Capital punishment for "a slave or a free person of color" was restricted to hanging.

1834

JUNE 2

Unionist judges John Belton O'Neall and David Johnson on the South Carolina Court of Appeals declared the militia oath void, because it violated the United States Constitution. William Harper dissented.

DECEMBER 17

The General Assembly passed legislation which incorporated the Saluda Manufacturing Company. Employing enslaved labor, it became the largest cotton factory in the state. It was burned by Union forces during the Civil War.

The General Assembly passed legislation which chartered the Bank of Charleston. It became the largest in the state at that time.

1835

APRIL

In New York, William Gilmore Simms published *The Yemassee* to great acclaim.

APRIL 1

The General Assembly passed legislation that made teaching literacy to free people of color and enslaved people illegal and subject to fines and imprisonment.

MAY

Daniel A. Payne closed his school for African Americans in Charleston and left the state.

JULY 29–30

A mob raided the Charleston post office in order to prevent the circulation of abolitionist pamphlets through the mails. Offending mailings were removed from the post office and burned.

Francis Lieber, the political philosopher, arrived in Columbia before October to begin twenty-one years of teaching at South Carolina College.

1836

Thomas Cooper and David J. McCord began to publish *The Statutes at Large of South Carolina* in ten volumes. The final volume was published in 1841.

FEBRUARY 4

Henry Laurens Pinckney presented resolutions in the United States House of Representatives which would become the "gag rule"— that any petition or paper involving the issue of slavery would be tabled and not discussed.

MAY 18

A select committee reported on Pinckney's resolutions, and the "gag rule" was adopted by a 117–68 vote.

SEPTEMBER–NOVEMBER

A major cholera epidemic ravaged Charleston.

NOVEMBER 3 – DECEMBER 7

Martin Van Buren defeated four other candidates for the presidency. South Carolina cast eleven electoral votes for Whig Willie P. Mangum of North Carolina.

1837

William Harper published his *Memoir on Slavery* as an antidote to abolitionist writings.

FEBRUARY 6

Calhoun defended slavery in a speech from the floor of the United States Senate as "a positive good."

MARCH 6

The Senate confirmed the appointment of Joel R. Poinsett as Secretary of War by President Van Buren.

1838

John Lyde Wilson published *The Code of Honor,* a handbook for conducting duels.

JANUARY 30

Osceola, the Seminole Indian chief, died in captivity at Fort Moultrie.

APRIL 27–28

Another great fire in Charleston destroyed nearly 150 acres at the heart of the commercial district—1,100 buildings total.

NOVEMBER 27

Angelica Singleton, daughter of Richard Singleton of Richland County, married Abram Van Buren, eldest son of President Martin Van Buren. The president being a widower, Angelica Singleton Van Buren often acted as First Lady.

1839

The General Synod of the Associate Reformed Presbyterian Church founded Erskine College, but did not obtain a state charter until 1850. The institution was the first four-year denominational college in South Carolina.

Theodore Weld published *American Slavery As It Is* with a number of stories drawn from the knowledge of the Grimké sisters (Weld and Angelina Grimké had married in 1838).

The College of Charleston became the first municipally funded college in the United States.

1840

US Census

White	259,084
Enslaved African American	327,038
Free African American	8,276
Total	594,398

The nation's first freestanding college library opened at South Carolina College. Robert Mills, the first federal architect, was closely involved in the design of what is now the South Caroliniana Library.

MARCH 13

The Nation Ford Treaty between the Catawba Indians and the state concluded in York District and would become the basis for the Catawba land suit in 1980.

OCTOBER 30-DECEMBER 2

William H. Harrison defeated Martin Van Buren for the presidency. South Carolina cast eleven electoral votes for Van Buren.

1841

Dr. N. P. Walker opened a school for the deaf at Cedar Springs near Spartanburg. The facility was expanded in 1855 to include education for the blind. In 1856 it became a state institution.

1842

JUNE 28

Railroad service between Charleston and Columbia began.

DECEMBER 20

The General Assembly passed legislation to convert the Arsenal at Columbia and the citadel and magazine in Charleston into a single South Carolina Military Academy. In 1845, the Arsenal Academy in Columbia became an auxiliary to the Citadel Academy in Charleston.

1844

The Methodists split into northern and southern churches over the question of whether a bishop might own slaves or not.

APRIL 10

President John Tyler appointed John C. Calhoun Secretary of State.

JULY 31

At a dinner in Bluffton in St. Luke's Parish, Robert Barnwell Rhett launched the Bluffton Movement for a state convention and separate state action on the tariff.

NOVEMBER 1–DECEMBER 4

James K. Polk defeated Henry Clay for the presidency. South Carolina cast nine electoral votes for Polk.

NOVEMBER 28

Judge Samuel Hoar of Massachusetts came to protest the Seamen's Acts but was driven out of the state.

1845

The Baptists in the nation split over the question of slavery.

DECEMBER 15

The General Assembly passed legislation granting, under William Gregg's direction, a charter to the Graniteville Manufacturing Company.

1846

MAY 13

The United States declared war on Mexico. South Carolina's Palmetto Regiment served with distinction.

AUGUST 8

David Wilmot of Pennsylvania urged a proviso to a wartime appropriations act stating that neither slavery nor involuntary servitude should exist in any territory acquired from Mexico.

1847

JANUARY 15

Robert B. Rhett in the United States House of Representatives opposed the Wilmot Proviso.

FEBRUARY 19

John C. Calhoun in the United States Senate opposed the Wilmot Proviso.

MARCH 9

The Palmetto Regiment landed at Tampico, Mexico. It suffered heavy casualties in several battles; only about half the men survived the war.

MAY

Daniel Webster made an extended visit to South Carolina and gave a public speech in Charleston May 8, an address to the New England Society May 10, an address to the Charleston Bar May 10, and an address to the students of South Carolina College May 17.

AUGUST 20

Former Gov. Pierce M. Butler was killed while leading the Palmetto Regiment at the Battle of Churubusco.

SEPTEMBER 13

The Palmetto flag was the first United States flag to be planted on the walls of Mexico City.

1848

Judge John Belton O'Neall completed codification of *The Negro Law of South Carolina*.

JULY

Workers completed the telegraph connection between Columbia and Charleston.

NOVEMBER 7

Zachary Taylor defeated Lewis Cass and Martin Van Buren for the presidency. South Carolina cast nine electoral votes for Cass.

1849

The German Colonization Society of Charleston, under the direction of John A. Wagener, purchased land for a German settlement at Walhalla.

JULY 13–14

After a massive jailbreak by enslaved people in Charleston, a mob threatened to burn the Episcopal Calvary Church, which was then being constructed to serve the Black community.

1850

US Census

White	274,563
Enslaved African American	384,984
Free African American	8,960
Total	668,507

MARCH 4

Too weak to stand and read the 42 pages himself, John C. Calhoun had Virginia Senator James Murray Mason read his final speech in the United States Senate in opposition to the Compromise of 1850 and with the hope of saving the Union. Calhoun would die March 31.

JUNE 3–12

Southern extremists met in convention at Nashville to condemn the Compromise of 1850 and promote Southern secession. Robert B. Rhett was the outspoken leader of the South Carolina delegation. When the second session met November 11–18, Langdon Cheves, a more moderate South Carolinian, spoke in favor of secession only if all southern states went out together.

DECEMBER 20

The General Assembly passed legislation which chartered Furman University, a Baptist institution. It opened in Greenville in 1852.

1851

DECEMBER 6

The General Assembly passed legislation that chartered Wofford College. A Methodist institution named for Benjamin Wofford, its first large benefactor, the school opened in Spartanburg in 1854.

FEBRUARY 10–11

An election was held for delegates to a state convention scheduled for April 1852 to consider separate state action.

MAY 5–8

The Southern Rights Association in favor of secession met in Charleston.

JULY 29

The Cooperationists, who would only secede if the South went as one, met in Charleston.

SEPTEMBER 23

A second meeting of the Cooperationists was held in Charleston.

OCTOBER 13–14

In this statewide election the people voted against separate state action. The state stepped back from the edge of secession.

DECEMBER 15

Workers laid the cornerstone for the third State House. This building, though substantially completed before the Civil War, was not completely finished until 1907.

1852

APRIL 26

The state convention which had been elected in February 1851 to consider separate state action met in Columbia.

JULY

Columbia and Greenville were joined by rail.

NOVEMBER 2

Franklin Pierce defeated Winfield Scott for the presidency. South Carolina cast nine electoral votes for Pierce.

1854

William Grayson's "The Hireling and the Slave" was published.

The South Carolina Baptist Convention established the Greenville Baptist Female College. In 1938 it merged with Furman University.

DECEMBER

James L. Petigru won a case for an alleged "low Yankee" abolitionist Reuben Smalle who had been abused by vigilantes in St. Bartholomew Parish.

1855

JUNE 2

The South Carolina Historical Society was established.

AUGUST 3

Architect John R. Niernsee began designing the new State House.

DECEMBER 19

The General Assembly passed legislation that established the Clarendon District, with the same boundaries as defined for the county in 1785.

1856

Charleston established a public school system that was modeled after New York schools.

MARCH 17

The Virginia legislature chartered the Mt. Vernon Ladies Association, organized by Ann Pamela Cunningham of Laurens County. She began the project in 1853 and the association purchased George Washington's home in 1858.

MAY 19

Massachusetts Senator Charles Sumner delivered his "The Crime against Kansas" speech in which he castigated South Carolina Senator Andrew Butler.

MAY 22

Congressman Preston Brooks, a nephew of Senator Butler, beat Charles Sumner thirty times over the head with a gutta percha walking cane as he sat at his desk in the United States Senate.

NOVEMBER

The first State Fair was held in Columbia.

NOVEMBER 4

James Buchanan defeated John C. Frémont and Millard Fillmore for the presidency. South Carolina cast eight electoral votes for Buchanan.

DECEMBER 20

The General Assembly passed legislation which chartered Newberry College, a Lutheran institution. It opened to students in 1859.

1857

DECEMBER 7

James L. Orr won election as Speaker of the United States House of Representatives.

1858

MARCH 4

Senator James Henry Hammond proclaimed "Cotton is King" during debates in the United States Senate.

1859

Columbia Female College (now called Columbia College), a Methodist institution, received its first students.

John Belton O'Neall published *Bench and Bar* in two volumes.

V

Secession, Rebellion, and Redemption (1860–1895)

In December 1860 South Carolina voted unanimously to secede from the Union. The state then sent commissioners to the other Southern states to urge them to secede and join in the formation of the Confederate States of America. Six followed South Carolina. The beginning of a civil war at Fort Sumter on April 14, 1861, brought four more Southern states into the Confederacy.

Except for the Sea Islands around Beaufort, South Carolina avoided federal occupation until Gen. William Tecumseh Sherman commenced his march of total war from Savannah to Columbia. Both Charleston and Columbia fell to federal troops on February 17, 1865.

The Civil War was a catastrophe for South Carolina. Not only were a large percentage of the men of the state killed or injured but also the economic and social system of nearly two centuries was wrecked forever. In its place developed Reconstruction, an era of both physical and ideological rebuilding of America. Slavery was abolished, African Americans were granted citizenship, and the right to vote was guaranteed for all men. In South Carolina, African Americans gained more political power than in any other state, and they and their white Republican allies helped bring the state closer to a semblance of true democracy than at any previous point in its history.

Much of the native white reaction to Reconstruction was negative. In the early 1870s conservatives began to regain some political strength, and by 1876, through a combination of legitimate electoral victories and violent suppression of African American and Republican voters, white Democrats had retaken control of the state.

When federal troops were withdrawn in 1877, white South Carolinians were given free rein to practice "home rule." Political power alternated uncertainly between representatives of the old gentry class on one hand, such as Wade Hampton, Duncan Clinch Heyward, and Richard I. Manning, who, moderate and reasonable as they were, could do little to revive the crippled economy, and flamboyant demagogues on the other hand, such as Ben Tillman and "Cole" Blease, who did incalculable harm by playing on the fears and resentments of the impoverished and demoralized whites.

During the 1880s textile mills, which had been present in the western part of the state since before the Civil War, grew into a major industry. The legal advancements made by African Americans during Reconstruction eroded. Many whites wished that the African Americans would simply go away, and they embodied their feelings in a complex system of racial segregation, one based in both law and custom. Acceptance of African American citizens' rights and place in the society was diminished by laws that resulted in their disenfranchisement and segregation. This process, which took place over the course of nearly two decades, culminated in the Constitution of 1895, which effectively eliminated African Americans from the political life of the state.

1860

US Census

White	291,300
Enslaved African American	402,406
Free African American	9,914
Other	88
Total	703,708

APRIL 16–17

The state Democratic convention met in Columbia to select delegates to attend the national Democratic convention that would be held in Charleston.

APRIL 23

The national Democratic convention met in Charleston. On April 28th, eight Southern delegations walked out in a dispute over the place of slavery in the party platform. South Carolina delegates remained.

NOVEMBER 1860–AUGUST 1865

Mary Boykin Chesnut of Camden kept a diary of her wartime life with commentary upon the times. The Chesnut Diary has become a Civil War classic.

NOVEMBER 6

Abraham Lincoln defeated John C. Breckinridge, John Bell, and Stephen Douglas for the presidency. South Carolina cast eight electoral votes for Breckinridge.

NOVEMBER 7

Federal District Judge Andrew Magrath and Federal District Attorney James Conner resigned their offices.

DECEMBER 6

The citizens voted on delegates to represent South Carolina at a Secession Convention.

DECEMBER 17

The Secession Convention opened in Columbia at the First Baptist Church but removed to Charleston because of fear of a smallpox outbreak in Columbia.

DECEMBER 20

The state of South Carolina "in convention assembled" at St. Andrews Hall in Charleston voted unanimously (169–0) to secede from the Union. The members signed the Ordinance of Secession the same evening in Institute Hall.

DECEMBER 26

Major Robert Anderson moved the federal troops in Charleston Harbor from Fort Moultrie to Fort Sumter.

1861

JANUARY 4

South Carolina sent secession commissioners to each Southern state.

JANUARY 9

The Citadel cadets stationed on Morris Island fired upon the US vessel *Star of the West*, which was bringing supplies to Fort Sumter.

FEBRUARY 9

South Carolina joined other Southern states in Montgomery, Alabama, to form the Confederate States of America.

MARCH 3

Gen. Pierre G. T. Beauregard arrived in Charleston to take command of the Confederate troops.

APRIL 12

Beauregard ordered the first shot fired on Fort Sumter.

APRIL 14

Anderson surrendered Fort Sumter to Beauregard. No lives had been lost in the battle.

APRIL 19

President Lincoln proclaimed a blockade of the Confederate ports.

MAY 11

With the arrival of the USS *Niagara*, the US naval blockade of Charleston began.

OCTOBER 12

Confederate commissioners James Mason and John Slidell left Charleston for Europe aboard the blockade runner *Theodora*.

NOVEMBER 7

The largest US fleet ever assembled to that point sailed past Hilton Head Island into Port Royal Sound. The planters abandoned the Sea Islands. The formerly enslaved people therefore became de facto freemen on, in their words, "the day of the big gun shoot."

DECEMBER 11

A great fire swept through Charleston from the Cooper River at East Bay north of the market to the corner of Tradd and Rutledge on the Ashley River.

DECEMBER 14

The Secession Convention reconvened and created an executive council that became the de facto government of the state. It was disbanded in December 1862.

DECEMBER 19–20

Union forces sank sixteen stone and granite loaded ships in Charleston harbor to obstruct passage. This "stone fleet" was augmented by an additional thirteen vessels sunk January 25–26, 1862.

1862

Penn Normal and Industrial School, founded at Frogmore on St. Helena Island by northern missionaries Laura Towne and Ellen Murray, began the education of African Americans on the Sea Islands.

MAY 13

Robert Smalls, an enslaved pilot, with an African American crew sailed in the Confederate steamer *Planter* out of Charleston and joined the Union fleet.

JUNE 16

The Confederates at Secessionville on James Island repulsed a Union attack.

OCTOBER 13

Gen. Ormsby Mitchel announced plans for a dedicated freedmen's village on Hilton Head Island. Mitchel would die October 30, but the town of Mitchelville, named in his honor, would become the first self-governing freedman's town.

NOVEMBER

The first African American regiment mustered into service in South Carolina. The First Regiment of South Carolina Volunteers was commanded by Col. Thomas W. Higginson, a white abolitionist from Massachusetts. During the war over 5,000 African Americans from South Carolina joined the Union Army.

1863

JANUARY 1

Lowcountry planter-turned-abolitionist William Henry Brisbane read aloud the Emancipation Proclamation at a celebration on the former Smith Plantation in Beaufort. It was the first public reading of the document in the South.

APRIL 7

Admiral Samuel Francis Du Pont attacked Fort Sumter.

JUNE 2

Harriet Tubman assisted Union troops in a raid up the Combahee River. The Union ships transported back to the Beaufort area more than 700 formerly enslaved people freed by the raid.

JULY 10

Union forces began an assault on Fort Wagner on Morris Island. Confederate forces evacuated the island September 6.

JULY 18

In the charge of the 54th Massachusetts against Fort Wagner, Col. Robert Gould Shaw fell as well as many formerly enslaved soldiers who were now fighting for their freedom.

AUGUST 22

The Swamp Angel, a gun on Morris Island, began to lob shells into the city of Charleston as far north as Calhoun Street.

OCTOBER 5

The Confederate submarine *David* attacked the USS *New Ironsides*.

OCTOBER 26–DECEMBER 6

The second great bombardment of Fort Sumter ensued unremitted for forty-one days and nights.

1864

FEBRUARY 17

The Confederate submarine *Hunley* sank the USS *Housatonic,* but it and its crew were also lost.

MAY 12

Wade Hampton assumed command of the Confederate Cavalry Corps upon the death of J. E. B. Stuart. He was not formally appointed until August 11.

JULY 7

The third and final great bombardment of Fort Sumter began.

DECEMBER

Andrew Gordon Magrath was elected the last governor under the state's 1790 constitution.

DECEMBER 24

Gen. William T. Sherman took Savannah.

1865

Daniel A. Payne returned to Charleston as the Bishop appointed to reestablish the African Methodist Episcopal Church in the state.

JANUARY–MARCH

Sherman marched through South Carolina from Savannah to North Carolina. In addition to the capital, twenty-one towns were in the path of the Union army.

JANUARY 16

Sherman issued Special Field Order No. 15, appropriating the Sea Islands and coastal lands for freedmen. Gen. Rufus Saxton was given the task of assigning the head of each family forty acres and the temporary use of a military horse or mule. This was probably the origin of the expression "forty acres and a mule."

FEBRUARY 3–4

The Battle of Rivers Bridge near Ehrhardt on the Salkehatchie River slowed the Union army's march to Columbia but cost approximately 200 Confederate and 400 Union casualties.

FEBRUARY 17

Federal troops took Charleston and Columbia the same day.

FEBRUARY 18

There was a great explosion at the Northeastern Railroad depot in Charleston.

Columbia burned.

MARCH 3

Congress established the Bureau of Refugees, Freedmen and Abandoned Lands. The life of the Freedmen's Bureau, as it was commonly called, was extended on July 18, 1866, and it functioned in South Carolina until June 30, 1872.

APRIL 5–21

Gen. Edward Potter led a Union raid into the interior of the state from Georgetown.

APRIL 9

Gen. Robert E. Lee surrendered the Army of Northern Virginia to Ulysses S. Grant at Appomattox Courthouse, Virginia. South Carolinian Martin W. Gary refused to surrender with Lee, delivered his command over to a subordinate, and shouted "South Carolinians never surrender" as he rode off the field.

APRIL 14

Robert Anderson raised the United States flag over Fort Sumter four years to the day after he surrendered. The Reverend Henry

Ward Beecher delivered the oration on that occasion, which was also attended by abolitionist William Lloyd Garrison, Robert Smalls, and Robert Vesey (son of Denmark), among others.

President Lincoln was assassinated in Washington, DC.

APRIL 16

African Americans in Charleston organized St. Mark's Episcopal Church.

MAY 2

Martin W. Gary and 200 men of his brigade led Jefferson Davis to his mother's house in Cokesbury, SC. Davis held the last Confederate council of war nearby at the home of Armistead Burt in Abbeville.

JUNE 30

President Andrew Johnson issued a proclamation establishing a provisional government for South Carolina. He named Benjamin F. Perry the provisional governor.

JULY 18

Maj. Gen. Quincy A. Gillmore assumed command of the military department of South Carolina.

SEPTEMBER 13–27

A convention met in Columbia and drew up the Constitution of 1865. The convention adopted the "Black Codes," considerably curtailing the freedom of former enslaved persons. Article XI abolished state offices in Charleston, thereby centralizing government in Columbia.

OCTOBER 1

Francis L. Cardozo established the Avery Normal Institute in Charleston.

NOVEMBER 13

South Carolina ratified the Thirteenth Amendment that outlawed slavery.

NOVEMBER 18

Gen. Daniel E. Sickles replaced Gillmore as commander of the Department of South Carolina.

NOVEMBER 29

James L. Orr was inaugurated governor under the Constitution of 1865.

1866

Dexter E. Converse became manager of the Converse Manufacturing Company near Spartanburg, a textile mill.

JANUARY 1

Gen. Sickles declared the "Black Codes" void.

SEPTEMBER

The General Assembly gave the crop-lien system legal sanction.

DECEMBER 19

South Carolina rejected the Fourteenth Amendment—the Senate unanimously and the House with but one vote for it.

DECEMBER 20

The General Assembly passed legislation to establish an immigration commissioner to encourage immigration of European whites to try to offset the African American majority.

1867

Phosphates were discovered in the Lowcountry and thus arose one of the state's first postwar industries.

MARCH 2

Congress established the Second Military District to consist of South Carolina and North Carolina with Maj. Gen. Daniel E. Sickles in command.

AUGUST 31

Maj. Gen. E. R. S. Canby succeeded Sickles in command of the Second District.

SEPTEMBER

The General Assembly authorized construction of the South Carolina Penitentiary at Columbia on the banks of the Congaree River. The facility accepted its first prisoner in 1867.

NOVEMBER 19–20

The first election in which the freedmen fully participated was held to elect state and local officials. The election lists provided the first records of the full names of freedmen.

1868

The Governor's Mansion, formerly the officers' quarters of the Arsenal Academy, became the official residence of the state's chief executive. Robert K. Scott was the first occupant.

JANUARY 14–MARCH 18

A convention drew up the Constitution of 1868. The convention was composed of seventy-six African Americans and forty-eight whites.

JANUARY 29

The General Assembly passed legislation that created Oconee County from the western half of Pickens County.

JUNE 2–3

Voters participated in the first general election held under the Constitution of 1868.

JULY 6

Gov. James L. Orr retired from the governorship to make way for Robert K. Scott of Ohio.

African Americans comprised a majority of the state legislators in 1868, the only state where this occurred, and no other state elected as many African Americans to local, state, or national offices during the Reconstruction era.

JULY 9

Francis L. Cardozo won election as the state's first African American Secretary of State.

JULY 9

South Carolina ratified the Fourteenth Amendment.

JULY 24

Military rule ended as Gen. Canby resigned his authority to the new civil government.

AUGUST 21

The General Assembly passed legislation that created Circuit Courts throughout the state.

NOVEMBER 3

Ulysses S. Grant defeated Horatio Seymour for election to the presidency. South Carolina cast six electoral votes for Grant.

1869

The Highland Park Hotel was built at Aiken and became an important destination for wealthy northern tourists.

DECEMBER 18

The General Assembly passed legislation that incorporated Claflin University, the state's oldest African American college, in Orangeburg.

1870

US Census

White	289,667
African American	415,814
Other	125
Total	**705,606**

Rhode Island native Bathsheba Benedict founded the Benedict Institute as a Baptist school with the goal of educating freedmen. The General Assembly granted it a charter as Benedict College in 1894.

FEBRUARY 1

Jonathan Jasper Wright won election as the first African American elected to the South Carolina Supreme Court. He served until his resignation December 1, 1877.

JULY 1

James W. Smith of South Carolina became the first African American student to enter the United States Military Academy at West Point.

NOVEMBER 28

Alonzo J. Ransier became the first African American from South Carolina to be elected to the office of Lieutenant Governor.

DECEMBER 12

Representative Joseph H. Rainey was the first African American from South Carolina to be sworn in as a member of the United States Congress.

1871

MARCH 6

The General Assembly passed a General School Act.

MARCH 10

The General Assembly created Aiken County from parts of Edgefield, Barnwell, Orangeburg, and Lexington counties.

MAY 9

The first Taxpayers Convention was held in Columbia.

MAY 24

The Patrons of Husbandry, or the Grange, was established in South Carolina with the organization of Ashley Grange No. 1 in Charleston.

OCTOBER 17

President Ulysses S. Grant issued a proclamation suspending the writ of habeas corpus in nine South Carolina counties under authority granted to him in the Ku Klux Klan Act April 20, 1871.

1872

The *Revised Statutes of South Carolina* were completed.

SEPTEMBER 21

John Henry Conyers was the first African American from South Carolina to enter the United States Naval Academy at Annapolis.

NOVEMBER 5

Ulysses S. Grant defeated Horace Greeley for the presidency. South Carolina cast seven electoral votes for Grant.

1873

OCTOBER 7

Secretary of State Henry E. Hayne was accepted as the first African American student at the University of South Carolina.

1874

JANUARY 6

African American Congressman Robert B. Elliott delivered a famous rebuttal to Alexander Stephens in support of the Civil Rights Act.

FEBRUARY 17

The second Taxpayers Convention was held in Columbia.

Daniel H. Chamberlain won election as governor.

1876

JULY 8

At least one white and six African Americans were killed in a race riot in the industrial town of Hamburg.

AUGUST 18

Pickens County Democrats held the state's first primary election.

SEPTEMBER 16–19

At least one white and about forty African Americans were killed in race riots at Ellenton in Aiken County.

OCTOBER 7

Gov. Daniel H. Chamberlain ordered the extralegal white militia "rifle clubs" to disband.

OCTOBER 17

President Grant issued a proclamation that placed federal troops at the call of Gov. Chamberlain.

NOVEMBER 7

The tempestuous and disputed gubernatorial election between the incumbent Chamberlain and Wade Hampton took place.

Rutherford B. Hayes defeated Samuel Tilden for the presidency. South Carolina's seven electoral votes were disputed but eventually counted for Hayes as part of the Compromise of 1877.

NOVEMBER 30–DECEMBER

Federal troops occupied the State House as Republicans and Democrats, both claiming victory in the House races, organized competing governments in the chamber.

DECEMBER 7

While Chamberlain was being inaugurated, Wade Hampton delivered a speech in which he said, "The people have elected me Governor, and by the Eternal God, I will be Governor or we shall have a military Governor."

DECEMBER 14

Wade Hampton, disputing Chamberlain's election, took the oath of office as governor.

Henry Martyn Robert published "Robert's Rules of Order."

1877

APRIL 10

President Hayes ordered federal troops withdrawn from Columbia. Under duress, Chamberlain conceded the gubernatorial dispute, leaving Hampton as governor.

JUNE 7

The Fence Law permitted enclosures, thus preventing cattle from grazing freely. It did not apply to the entire state until 1921.

The General Assembly moved to end African American admissions to the University of South Carolina by closing the University. It would not reopen until 1880, this time as an all-white college of agricultural and mechanical arts.

1878

FEBRUARY 18

The General Assembly passed legislation that created Hampton County from part of Beaufort County.

MARCH 1

The General Assembly passed legislation to end public executions.

APRIL 18

The *Azor,* carrying 206 African American Carolinians, sailed for Liberia.

DECEMBER 10

Wade Hampton won election to the United States Senate.

DECEMBER 23

The General Assembly passed legislation that established the State Board of Health.

DECEMBER 24

The General Assembly passed legislation that established the State Railroad Commission.

1880

US Census

White	391,105
African American	604,332
Other	140
Total	995,577

The 1880 census was the only federal census in which the state's Black population exceeded 60 percent.

Sallie Flournoy Moore organized the first local chapter of the Women's Christian Temperance Union in South Carolina.

JULY 5

W. M. Shannon was killed in a duel by E. B. C. Cash. Legislation enacted in December 1880 made dueling henceforth a crime.

NOVEMBER 2

James A. Garfield defeated Winfield Scott Hancock for the presidency. South Carolina cast seven electoral votes for Hancock.

DECEMBER 24

The General Assembly granted a charter to Allen University, an African Methodist Episcopal institution.

1881

Charleston investors Francis Pelzer and Ellison Smyth established the Pelzer Manufacturing Company on the Saluda River in Anderson County.

1882

JANUARY 30

The General Assembly passed legislation that created Berkeley County from a part of Charleston County.

The Pacolet Manufacturing Company was founded by John H. Montgomery and C. E. Fleming. It initiated a much greater involvement of New England and New York engineering, machinery, and commission house business in the South Carolina textile industry.

FEBRUARY 9

The General Assembly passed legislation employing an "Eight Box Voting law" to reduce African American participation.

JULY 5

The "Dibble Plan" created one large Lowcountry district (the "Black Seventh") to diminish the number of African American voters in other districts.

1884

MAY

The University of South Carolina Law School reopened with Joseph D. Pope as head.

NOVEMBER 4

Grover Cleveland defeated James G. Blaine for the Presidency. South Carolina cast nine electoral votes for Cleveland.

DECEMBER 11

The General Assembly passed legislation that incorporated the South Carolina Bar Association.

1885

AUGUST 6

Benjamin Ryan Tillman made a stunning speech on the plight of the farmer at Bennettsville before the State Grange and the State Agricultural and Mechanical Society.

1886

AUGUST 31

Ninety-two people died in an earthquake that caused enormous property damage in Charleston.

DECEMBER 23

The General Assembly passed a general incorporation law.

1888

NOVEMBER 6

Benjamin Harrison defeated Grover Cleveland for the presidency. South Carolina cast nine electoral votes for Cleveland.

DECEMBER 22

The General Assembly passed legislation that created Florence County from parts of Marion, Darlington, Williamsburg, and Clarendon counties.

1889

A group of Spartanburg citizens founded Converse College for the education of women. It opened to students October 1, 1890.

MAY 21

The Federal Circuit Court of Appeals validated the will of Thomas G. Clemson who had left money for the founding of an institution of higher learning at the former home of John C. Calhoun.

DECEMBER 14

Wofford defeated Furman five goals to one in the state's first intercollegiate football game.

1890

US Census

White	462,008
African American	688,934
Other	207
Total	**1,151,149**

JANUARY 23

The "Shell Manifesto," written by Ben Tillman, issued a call for a convention of the Farmers' Movement.

NOVEMBER 3

In the "Revolution of 1890" Tillman populists defeated the aristocratic old guard at the polls.

DECEMBER 11

The Tillman-controlled state legislature selected John L. M. Irby to replace Wade Hampton in the US Senate.

1891

FEBRUARY 18

The first issue of *The State* was issued with N. G. Gonzales as manager and editor.

JUNE

The United States Marine Corps established a training base on Parris Island.

1892

FEBRUARY

The National Board of the Society of the Daughters of the American Revolution (DAR) elected Rebecca Pickens Bacon as State Regent. In May, State of South Carolina organized its first DAR chapter in Columbia.

NOVEMBER 8

Grover Cleveland defeated Benjamin Harrison and James B. Weaver for the presidency. South Carolina cast nine electoral votes for Cleveland.

DECEMBER 24

The legislature limited the hours of work in cotton and woolen factories to sixty-six per week or eleven a day.

DECEMBER 24

The Dispensary system of selling liquor went into effect. This state monopoly lasted until 1907.

1893

JANUARY 21

The General Assembly passed legislation that chartered the Columbia Mills Company with an initial capitalization of $700,000. It would be the nation's first totally electrified textile plant. In 1981 the building was donated to the state to house the State Museum.

JULY 6

Clemson College received its first students.

AUGUST 27 AND OCTOBER 13

Severe hurricanes swept the state; over 1,000 lives were lost in the coastal areas.

1894

OCTOBER

Sara Campbell Allen became the first woman physician in South Carolina.

President Grover Cleveland came to Georgetown to shoot ducks. When a stiff gale overturned his skiff, national attention focused upon South Carolina as a hunting preserve. Wealthy Northern sportsmen began to come south for the winter.

MARCH 30

In Darlington there was a riot between constables who were enforcing the new liquor laws and local citizens who resented their doing so.

NOVEMBER 6

George Washington Murray was elected to the United States House of Representatives. He would be South Carolina's last African American Congressman until 1992.

NOVEMBER 7

The state's first chapter of the United Daughters of the Confederacy organized.

1895

Construction began on Olympia Mill in Columbia. Upon completion it contained over 100,000 spindles, the world's largest textile mill under one roof.

MARCH 4

Tillman entered the United States Senate, where he sat until his death on July 3, 1918.

SEPTEMBER 10–DECEMBER 4

A convention drafted the Constitution of 1895. It defined a "Negro" as one who had $1/8$ or more African American ancestry.

SEPTEMBER 24

Frances Guignard Gibbes of Columbia became the first woman allowed to take a course at the University of South Carolina. Three years later, Mattie Jean Adams became the first woman to graduate from the University.

OCTOBER 15

Winthrop Normal College for Women in Rock Hill, created by the state legislature in 1891, received its first students.

OCTOBER 25

Thomas E. Miller, one of six African American delegates, addressed the Constitutional Convention in support of unrestricted suffrage.

DECEMBER 4

The convention adopted the Constitution of 1895, but it was not sent to the people for ratification.

VI

A Segregated South Carolina
(1896–1964)

Exhausted soils, hurricanes, the boll weevil, and a general depression in the prices of agricultural products kept South Carolina poor when other sections of the nation were prospering.
Indeed, the rest of the nation joined South Carolina in its economic
struggles in 1930. A severe economic depression, which followed the
stock market crash in 1929, brought the American standard of living
down to the point where the chronic poverty of South Carolina was
no longer so remarkable.

In politics, the energetic James F. Byrnes was elected to the United
States Senate. In 1932 a Democrat with some Southern sympathies,
Franklin Delano Roosevelt, was elected president, and thus the Democratic Party of South Carolina became a branch of a nationwide political party that was in power.

The federal government poured money into the state, many public works were undertaken, pellagra was virtually eliminated, malaria
greatly reduced, and hookworm infestation curbed. In World War
II, rising prices for farm products and war-related industrialization
brought prosperity to the state for the first time since before the Civil
War.

After the war African Americans were no longer willing to accept
the most extreme indignities of segregation. While impetuous whites
wasted their energies in futile attempts to resist the achievement of civil
rights for African Americans, more moderate leaders generally prevented violent confrontations. After the famous 1954 Supreme Court
decision, which began the end of segregation in the schools, the state
needed more than ten years to adjust. Clemson University admitted

Harvey Gantt in 1963 as its first African American student, and by the end of 1964 the University of South Carolina had opened its doors to all of the state's citizens. The Civil Rights Acts of 1964 and 1965 and the Voting Rights Act of 1965 marked the beginning of a new era.

The computer revolution also began in the middle of the 1960s, speeding up the rate of change in banking, business, and government affairs. In the 1960s the leadership in the state was extraordinarily successful in attracting new business to the state, especially foreign-owned industries, which introduced a cosmopolitan awareness into the state's social and intellectual life. Air-conditioning improved summer working conditions, which eased some of the tensions in the rapidly industrializing state.

1896

FEBRUARY 25

The General Assembly passed legislation that created Saluda County from part of Edgefield County.

MARCH 3

The General Assembly established the State College for Negroes at Orangeburg. Former Congressman Thomas E. Miller served as its first president.

MAY 28

The United States Supreme Court in *Plessy v. Ferguson* upheld "separate but equal" segregation.

AUGUST 25

South Carolina held the nation's first statewide primary election.

NOVEMBER 3

William McKinley defeated William Jennings Bryan for the presidency. South Carolina cast nine electoral votes for Bryan.

NOVEMBER 12

The University of South Carolina defeated Clemson 12–6 in the first "Big Thursday" football game.

1897

Voorhees Normal and Industrial School, founded at Denmark by Elizabeth Evelyn Wright, was named for benefactor Ralph Voorhees.

General Hospital opened in Columbia. Dr. Matilda Arabelle Evans, who graduated from the Women's Medical College of Pennsylvania that year, established this the first African American hospital in Columbia. She became the first female physician in Columbia and the first South Carolina African American woman to practice medicine in the state.

The first volume of Edward McCrady's four-volume history of South Carolina was published.

FEBRUARY 25

The General Assembly passed legislation that organized Bamberg, Cherokee, and Dorchester counties.

MARCH 2

The General Assembly passed legislation that created Greenwood County from parts of Abbeville and Edgefield counties.

MARCH 5

The General Assembly enacted legislation providing for a state income tax.

1898

FEBRUARY 19

The General Assembly passed legislation, in the spirit of *Plessy v. Ferguson,* that separate coaches for whites and African Americans were required on all railroads operating in South Carolina.

APRIL 25

The United States declared war on Spain. Many South Carolinians volunteered for service in the Spanish-American War.

NOVEMBER 8

The state's last election day riot took place in Phoenix, in Greenwood County, and resulted in the deaths of one white and seven African Americans.

1899

Writer and women's suffrage advocate Virginia Durant Young became sole owner of the Fairfax *Enterprise.*

The company that would evolve into Sonoco Products was established at Hartsville to manufacture paper cones used in the growing textile industry.

1900

US Census

	White	557,807
	African American	782,321
	Other	188
	Total	**1,340,316**

SEPTEMBER 29–OCTOBER 2

Race riots in Georgetown ended the Reconstruction practice of having a "fusion" ticket, whereby political offices were divided between African Americans and whites.

NOVEMBER 6

William McKinley defeated William Jennings Bryan for the presidency. South Carolina cast nine electoral votes for Bryan.

1901

DECEMBER 1–MAY 31, 1902

The Interstate and West Indian Exposition was held in Charleston.

1902

FEBRUARY 22

In the United States Senate chamber, Tillman assaulted the state's moderate and progressive Senator John L. McLaurin.

FEBRUARY 25

The General Assembly passed legislation that created Lee County from Darlington, Kershaw, and Sumter counties.

1903

JANUARY 5

Theodore Roosevelt appointed an African American man, Dr. William D. Crum, collector of the Port of Charleston.

JANUARY 15

Lt. Gov. James H. Tillman, nephew of Ben Tillman, shot and killed N. G. Gonzales, editor of *The State*. A Lexington County jury (after a change of venue) found Tillman not guilty.

FEBRUARY 13

The General Assembly passed the state's first child labor law, introduced by Richland County Senator J. Q. Marshall. As of May 1,

1903, no child under ten years of age could be employed in a factory, mine, or mill in the state. As of May 1, 1904, it would be eleven years, and as of May 1, 1905, twelve years of age.

JUNE 6

A great flood on the Pacolet River took over sixty lives.

1904

Lander Academy for women, a Methodist institution, moved from Williamston to Greenwood and renamed Lander College. In 1951 Greenwood County assumed operation of the school and on July 1, 1973, Lander became a state supported college.

NOVEMBER 8

Theodore Roosevelt defeated Alton B. Parker for the presidency. South Carolina cast nine electoral votes for Parker.

1905

Gibbes Art Gallery, built with a bequest by Charleston merchant James S. Gibbes, opened.

Bernard Baruch recreated Hobcaw Barony.

1907

FEBRUARY 16

The General Assembly passed legislation that abolished the corrupt and controversial state Dispensary system.

FEBRUARY 19

The General Assembly passed legislation that provided for full secondary education throughout the state for white students.

1908

FEBRUARY 14

The General Assembly passed legislation that created Calhoun County from parts of Orangeburg and Lexington counties.

NOVEMBER 3

William H. Taft defeated William Jennings Bryan for the presidency. South Carolina cast nine electoral votes for Bryan.

Ellison Durant ("Cotton Ed") Smith was elected to the United States Senate, where he continued to sit until his death on November 17, 1944.

1909

South Carolina Federation of Colored Women's Clubs was organized.

1910

US Census

White	679,161
African American	833,843
Other	396
Total	1,515,400

FEBRUARY 5

The General Assembly passed legislation that created Dillon County from Marion County.

FEBRUARY 26

The General Assembly passed legislation that created the State Board of Law Examiners.

NOVEMBER 8

Coleman L. ("Cole") Blease was elected governor on a platform of extreme race hatred and disgust with the white elite.

1911

FEBRUARY 11

The General Assembly passed a concurrent resolution that designated Henry Timrod's "Carolina" as the state song.

AUGUST 27

A severe hurricane wiped out the last attempts to grow rice commercially in the state.

1912

JANUARY 30

The General Assembly passed legislation that created Jasper County from parts of Beaufort and Hampton counties.

NOVEMBER 5

Woodrow Wilson defeated Theodore Roosevelt, William Howard Taft, and Eugene V. Debs for the presidency. South Carolina cast nine electoral votes for Wilson.

1914

David R. Coker founded the Coker Pedigree Seed Company.

In Columbia, "The University Press" (later called the University of South Carolina Press) began publishing scholarly monographs.

JULY

A wildcat strike at Lewis Parker's Monaghan Mill in Greenville erupted into a major confrontation. The workers were organized by the Industrial Workers of the World.

AUGUST 3

Germany declared war on France.

1915

FEBRUARY 20

The General Assembly passed legislation that established the State Tax Commission.

FEBRUARY 20

The General Assembly passed legislation that established compulsory education. The Act became effective July 1, 1915, and applied to children eight to fourteen years of age.

FEBRUARY 20

Under the new governor, Richard I. Manning, modern social-welfare legislation in South Carolina began with the establishment of the State Board of Charities and Corrections.

OCTOBER 21

The film "Birth of a Nation," a skewed portrayal of Reconstruction in South Carolina, premiered in the state.

1916

JANUARY

The first Anderson car was built at Rock Hill by John Gary Anderson. Although this was the South's most successful automobile, the firm went bankrupt within a decade.

JANUARY 1

Statewide prohibition went into effect following a 1915 referendum whereby South Carolina voted to prohibit the sale of all alcoholic beverages.

FEBRUARY 19

The General Assembly passed legislation that created McCormick County from portions of Abbeville, Edgefield, and Greenwood counties.

FEBRUARY 29

A Child Labor Law raised the minimum age for employment to fourteen.

JULY

The great flood of 1916 swept down from the mountains of North Carolina and was especially destructive in the Pee Dee.

1917

Cotton farmers first detected the boll weevil in South Carolina.

FEBRUARY 20

The General Assembly passed legislation that established the State Highway Department. Henceforth, licenses were required for all motor vehicles. The state took responsibility for a state road system.

FEBRUARY 27

Activists founded the first South Carolina chapter of the NAACP at Charleston with portrait painter and businessman Edwin A. Harleston as its president.

APRIL 6

The United States entered World War I and Gov. Manning appointed a Commission on Civic Preparedness for War (chairman David R. Coker). Shortly thereafter officials established National Guard camps outside Greenville and Spartanburg, located a US Army camp near Columbia, and expanded the navy yard near Charleston.

JULY 18

The War Department named the US Army camp on former Hampton property on the eastern edge of Columbia Camp Jackson, in honor of Andrew Jackson.

1918

FEBRUARY 14

The General Assembly passed legislation that permitted women to practice law in the state. James M. "Miss Jim" Perry became the first South Carolina woman admitted to the Bar.

SEPTEMBER 30

The College of Charleston admitted its first women.

OCTOBER

An influenza epidemic, which reached its height with 4,274 deaths that month, resulted in 170,000 cases and 7,400 deaths in South Carolina.

NOVEMBER 11

World War I came to an end following the signing of an armistice between the Allies and Germany. 62,000 South Carolinians had served during the conflict. Eight South Carolinians were awarded the Medal of Honor.

1919

The boll weevil destroyed 90 percent of the Sea Island cotton crop. Cotton was never again grown successfully on a commercial scale in the Sea Islands.

JANUARY

An African American convention at Columbia, with representatives from across the state, challenged the state's system of segregation and voting restrictions and called for better education and representation on school boards.

FEBRUARY 6

The General Assembly passed legislation that created Allendale County from Barnwell and Hampton counties.

OCTOBER 9

Town Theater, the oldest surviving community theater in the country, offered its first productions in the Columbia High School auditorium.

1920

US Census

	White	818,538
	African American	864,719
	Other	467
	Total	1,683,724

APRIL 21

Community leaders held the first meeting to organize the Society for the Preservation of Old Dwellings in Charleston.

SEPTEMBER

African American teachers replaced white teachers in Charleston's African American public schools in response to an NAACP-organized campaign.

NOVEMBER 2

Women voted for the first time in the state after the adoption of the Nineteenth Amendment (August 26, 1920). South Carolina, however, did not ratify the amendment until 1969.

NOVEMBER 2

Warren G. Harding defeated James M. Cox for the presidency. South Carolina cast nine electoral votes for Cox.

1921

A long agricultural depression began.

In Charleston, the Poetry Society published its first yearbook.

Wil Lou Gray helped launch the Opportunity School as an adult education program.

AUGUST 3

Judge Kenesaw Mountain Landis instituted a lifetime ban from Major League Baseball for "Shoeless" Joe Jackson of Greenville for allegedly participating in the 1919 "Black Sox" scandal.

1922

AUGUST 20

Lucile Ellerbe Godbold won an Olympic gold medal in track and field. She was the first woman named to the South Carolina Athletic Hall of Fame.

MARCH 15

The General Assembly passed legislation that limited the hours of work in textile mills to ten hours a day or fifty-five hours a week.

1923

For the first time in over a century whites outnumbered African Americans in South Carolina. The proportion of African Americans had declined following 1880, with their increasing emigration to the North and Midwest.

MAY 17

A fire at Cleveland School, near Camden, claimed seventy lives.

OCTOBER 29

The musical "Runnin' Wild" opened on Broadway, introducing the dance known as "The Charleston."

1924

MARCH 21

The General Assembly passed legislation establishing the "6-0-1" school law, whereby the state would pay a teacher's salary for six months if the county would pay for one month.

FEBRUARY 1

The General Assembly adopted yellow jessamine (*Gelsemium sempervirens*) as the state flower.

NOVEMBER 4

Calvin Coolidge defeated John W. Davis and Robert M. LaFollette for the presidency. South Carolina cast nine electoral votes for Davis.

1926

The development of Myrtle Beach as a resort began with the opening of John T. Woodside's Ocean Forest Hotel.

1927

APRIL 26

The General Assembly passed legislation that established the State Forestry Commission.

1928

JUNE 28

The Congaree River (Gervais Street) Bridge, connecting Columbia and West Columbia, opened to traffic.

NOVEMBER 6

Mrs. Mary Gordon Ellis won election as senator for Jasper County, the first woman elected to the South Carolina legislature.

NOVEMBER 6

Herbert Hoover defeated Alfred E. Smith for the presidency. South Carolina cast nine electoral votes for Smith.

1929

The South Carolina Legislature held hearings on labor conditions and concluded that textile workers had valid complaints against management.

MARCH 14

The legislature authorized an unprecedented $65 million bond issue, of doubtful constitutionality, to complete the state highway system.

MAY 24

Julia Peterkin's novel *Scarlet Sister Mary* won the Pulitzer Prize.

AUGUST 8

The Cooper River Bridge, joining Charleston and Mount Pleasant, opened to traffic. The two-mile-long bridge (with a main span of 1,050 feet and a vertical clearance of 150 feet) was one of the longest highway bridges in the world.

SEPTEMBER 20

Columbia's Owens Field airport opened to commercial passengers.

OCTOBER 29

In New York, prices collapsed on the New York Stock Exchange.

1930

US Census

White	944,049
African American	793,681
Other	1,035
Total	1,738,765

FEBRUARY 13

WSPA-Spartanburg initiated the first radio broadcast in the state.

APRIL 4

The General Assembly passed legislation establishing the state Highway Patrol and established a system of driver licensing.

JULY

Lake Murray came into existence when its reservoir reached an elevation of 298.5 feet behind the Dreher Shoals Dam on the Saluda

River in Lexington County, then the largest earthen dam in the world for hydroelectricity.

NOVEMBER 4

James F. Byrnes defeated "Cole" Blease for the United States Senate. Byrnes, who became the state's most influential representative in Washington since Calhoun, sat in the Senate until he was appointed to the United States Supreme Court in 1941.

DECEMBER 1

The first electric power was delivered to Duke Power Company from the Dreher Shoals Dam.

1931

Sculptor Anna Vaughan Hyatt Huntington and her husband Archer Milton Huntington founded Brookgreen Gardens near Georgetown.

OCTOBER 13

The Charleston City Council passed the nation's first Historic Preservation ordinance.

DECEMBER 31

The failure of People's State Bank began a run on other banks.

1932

NOVEMBER 8

Franklin D. Roosevelt defeated Herbert Hoover for the presidency. South Carolina cast eight electoral votes for Roosevelt. (He received almost 98 percent of the state's popular vote.)

A constitutional amendment, implemented by legislation the following year, changed South Carolina's fiscal year from January 1–December 31 to July 1–June 30.

1933

DECEMBER 5

The Twenty-First Amendment repealed the Eighteenth Amendment and ended national prohibition. South Carolina, however, legalized only beer and wine, still forbidding the sale of strong liquors under the 1915 laws.

1934

The US Soil Erosion Service began planting kudzu in Spartanburg County.

MAY 19

Gov. Ibra C. Blackwood signed the Act which created the South Carolina Public Service Authority, which was to build the Santee-Cooper dams.

SEPTEMBER 1–22

About 45,000 of the state's 80,000 textile workers actively participated in the United Textile Workers (A. F. of L.) strike. Seven workers were shot and killed by special deputies at Chiquola Mills at Honea Path.

1935

David Duncan Wallace's *History of South Carolina* was completed with the publication of the final two volumes of the four volume work.

MAY 14

With the end of national prohibition, the South Carolina General Assembly passed an alcoholic beverage control law to regulate the sale of liquor.

OCTOBER 10

George Gershwin's opera *Porgy and Bess,* with words by Ira Gershwin based on South Carolinian DuBose Heyward's novel *Porgy,* received its first performance at the Alvin Theater in New York City.

OCTOBER 28

A constitutional crisis arose when Gov. Olin D. Johnston proclaimed the State Highway Department in rebellion and ordered the National Guard to occupy its offices. No irregularities were found in the operations of the department, which ran itself with exemplary efficiency but which was politically independent and insensitive.

1936

President Roosevelt appointed Mary McLeod Bethune of Mayesville Director of Negro Affairs within the National Youth Administration. She thus became the first African American female division head in the federal government and member of the unofficial "Black Cabinet."

MAY

Appointment of highway commissioners was placed in the hands of the legislature (previously the commissioners had been appointed by the governor for staggered terms).

JUNE 25

Senator "Cotton Ed" Smith walked out of the Democratic National Convention in protest when an African American clergyman was selected to offer an invocation.

NOVEMBER 3

Franklin D. Roosevelt defeated Alf Landon for the presidency. South Carolina cast eight electoral votes for Roosevelt.

1937

FEBRUARY 24

The South Caroliniana Society held its first annual meeting in Columbia.

MAY 13

The General Assembly passed the South Carolina Public Welfare Act to implement the national Social Security Act, providing aid for the blind, aged, and disabled.

NOVEMBER 26

The new Dock Street Theatre, constructed on the site of the original playhouse with a combination of local and WPA funds, opened with a performance of "The Recruiting Officer."

DECEMBER 12

A riot at the state penitentiary in Columbia left one officer dead. Six inmates were convicted in the death and all were executed March 24, 1939.

1938

MARCH 12

The General Assembly passed legislation which established the State Planning Board. It evolved into the State Development Board.

JUNE 14–AUGUST 30

The most colorful primary in the history of the state pitted "Cotton Ed" Smith, Olin D. Johnston, and Edgar Brown against each other for the United States Senate. Smith won.

SEPTEMBER 20

Two tornadoes struck Charleston, killing twenty-nine people.

NOVEMBER 8

Burnet Maybank became the first Charlestonian since the Civil War to be elected governor.

1939

JANUARY 28

The "air cooled" Riviera Theater opened in Charleston.

MARCH 17

The General Assembly officially adopted the palmetto as the state tree.

APRIL 18

The clearing of land for the Santee-Cooper dams and powerhouses began.

SEPTEMBER 1

In Europe, World War II began with the German invasion of Poland.

1940

US Census

White	1,084,308
African American	814,164
Other	1,332
Total	1,899,804

JUNE

The reactivated Camp Jackson became Fort Jackson, a permanent army post.

AUGUST 11

A hurricane tore through Beaufort, Edisto Island, and Charleston, killing at least forty people.

NOVEMBER 5

Franklin D. Roosevelt defeated Wendell Willkie for reelection to the presidency. South Carolina cast eight electoral votes for Roosevelt.

1941

In New York, Wilbur J. Cash's *The Mind of the South* was published.

MARCH 17

David Edward Finley, of York, oversaw the opening of the National Gallery of Art as its first director.

JULY 7

James F. Byrnes took his oath as an Associate Justice of the United States Supreme Court.

DECEMBER 11

Cassandra Maxwell of Orangeburg became the first African American woman admitted to the South Carolina Bar.

1942

Annie Greene Nelson published her first novel, *After the Storm.*

MARCH 5

The General Assembly passed legislation that established the State Ports Authority.

APRIL 18

Gen. Jimmy Doolittle led a squadron of B-25s, made up of crews from the Columbia Army Air Base, in a bombing raid on Tokyo.

OCTOBER 3

James F. Byrnes resigned from the United States Supreme Court to become Director of Office of Economic Stabilization.

DECEMBER 2

The Santee-Cooper project, a rural electrification and public works project undertaken as part of the New Deal and which resulted in the creation of Lakes Marion and Moultrie, was substantially complete. It was the single largest New Deal project undertaken in South Carolina and at the time represented the largest land clearing project in United States history.

1943

MAY 27

President Roosevelt appointed James F. Byrnes Director the Office of War Mobilization. Byrnes acquired the reputation of being "assistant president."

1944

African Americans organized the Progressive Democratic Party to encourage political activity in the African American community and to pressure the state Democratic Party to admit African American members.

APRIL 3

The United States Supreme Court, in the *Smith v Allwright* decision, ruled the state-run white-only Democratic primary illegal for denying African American citizens the right to vote in primary elections.

APRIL 14

Gov. Olin D. Johnston called a special session of the General Assembly to separate party primaries from state control. The legislature responded by enacting 147 laws in six days to exclude African American voters by allowing political parties to hold primaries as private organizations.

JULY 19–20

Byrnes was overlooked as the Democratic Vice-Presidential nominee because of opposition from labor and African American leaders.

NOVEMBER 7

Franklin D. Roosevelt defeated Thomas E. Dewey for reelection to the presidency. South Carolina cast eight electoral votes for Roosevelt.

1945

AUGUST 15

World War II ended. Over 170,000 South Carolinians served during the war

OCTOBER

Striking African American tobacco workers in Charleston first sang the song "I'll Overcome Some Day." By the end of the strike, the lyrics had been changed to "We Shall Overcome," and the song would eventually become the anthem of the Civil Rights Movement.

1946

NOVEMBER 4

Strom Thurmond won election as governor.

1947

FEBRUARY 16

A mob seized Willie Earle from the Pickens County jail and murdered him. This lynching attracted national and international attention. All thirty-one white defendants were acquitted in the subsequent Greenville trial.

JULY 12

Judge Waites Waring issued his decision in *Elmore v. Rice* that brought an end to the all-white Democratic primary.

1948

JULY 17

Dissident Southern Democrats or "Dixiecrats" convened in Birmingham where they nominated Strom Thurmond as the presidential candidate of their States' Rights Party.

NOVEMBER 2

Harry Truman defeated Thomas E. Dewey and Strom Thurmond for the presidency. South Carolina cast eight electoral votes for Thurmond. Thurmond collected thirty-nine electoral votes in all, carried four Deep South states, and received 2.4% of the popular vote (1,175,930 total votes).

DECEMBER 6

The Greenville Symphony gave its first performance.

1949

The eighteen story Cornell Arms apartment building in Columbia became the state's first "skyscraper." At the time of its completion, the complex was the tallest building between Richmond and Miami.

APRIL 4

Marian Anderson performed before a segregated audience at the Columbia Township Auditorium.

APRIL 15

The General Assembly ratified a state constitutional amendment that permitted divorce on the grounds of adultery, desertion, physical cruelty, or habitual drunkenness; previously divorce was not granted on any grounds.

OCTOBER

David Edward Finley founded the National Trust for Historic Preservation.

NOVEMBER 11

African American parents with the assistance of the NAACP alleged the segregated Clarendon County school system discriminated against their children. Their suit eventually became part of the *Brown v. Board of Education of Topeka* case.

1950

US Census

White	1,293,405
African American	822,077
Other	1,545
Total	2,117,027

The State Budget and Control Board replaced the Budget Commission. Under a reorganization plan adopted by the Assembly, ten state agencies were abolished, and their functions and duties were assumed by the Budget and Control Board.

The Dupont Corporation opened the May chemical plant in Camden.

MARCH 23

The Columbia Museum of Art opened to the public.

SEPTEMBER 4

The first Southern 500 NASCAR race took place at the Darlington Raceway.

NOVEMBER 28

The Atomic Energy Commission and Dupont selected a 250,000-acre site in Aiken and Barnwell counties for the Savannah River plant. It was created to produce plutonium and tritium, elements used in nuclear weapons. The facility would become one of the largest employers in the state but also a focal point for anti-nuclear power protestors and environmental activists.

1951

MARCH 12

The South Carolina Philharmonic Orchestra gave its first performance.

APRIL 15

Gov. James F. Byrnes instituted a $75 million program to make African American schools "equal" to white schools in an effort to forestall racial integration of the South Carolina's public schools. A three percent sales tax, the first in the history of the state, was levied to finance the program.

1952

NOVEMBER 4

Voters approved an amendment to the state constitution empowering the legislature to close public schools, if necessary, to avoid integration.

Dwight Eisenhower defeated Adlai Stevenson for the presidency. South Carolina cast eight electoral votes for Stevenson.

1953

MAY 1

The state's first television station, WCOS-TV Columbia, began broadcasting.

1954

MARCH 19

The General Assembly passed "Right to Work" legislation which outlawed the closed shop.

MAY 17

The US Supreme Court, in *Brown v. Board of Education of Topeka*, ruled that "separate but equal" schools were unconstitutional.

NOVEMBER 2

Strom Thurmond won election to the United States Senate on a write-in vote, defeating the regular candidate of the Democratic Party, State Senator Edgar Brown.

1956

JANUARY 10–APRIL 10

The General Assembly, in its "segregation session," passed laws to avoid integration by circumventing recent Supreme Court rulings.

SEPTEMBER 8

Marian McKnight was crowned Miss America for 1957.

NOVEMBER 6

Dwight Eisenhower defeated Adlai Stevenson for reelection to the presidency. South Carolina cast eight electoral votes for Stevenson.

1957

Althea Gibson became the first South Carolinian as well as the first African American to compete at Wimbledon and, in 1958, the first African American woman to win the Wimbledon title.

1958

JANUARY

Jasper Johns' one-man exhibition at Leo Castelli's New York Gallery helped launch the Pop Art movement.

SEPTEMBER

Experimental classroom use of television at Columbia's Dreher High School led to the establishment of South Carolina Educational Television (SCETV) in 1960.

1960

US Census

White	1,551,022
African American	829,291
Native American	1,098
Japanese	460
Chinese	158
Filipino	328
Other	237
Total	2,382,594

JANUARY 1

The first modern civil rights demonstration in South Carolina took place when African Americans marched to the Greenville airport to protest the segregated waiting rooms. The march had been pro-voked when baseball star Jackie Robinson was insulted and threat-ened with arrest for entering the "white" waiting room.

FEBRUARY 12

The term "sit-in" began to be used when about 100 African Ameri-can students from Friendship Junior College in Rock Hill entered two of the city's largest variety stores and requested service at the segregated lunch counters.

NOVEMBER 8

John F. Kennedy defeated Richard Nixon for the presidency. South Carolina cast eight electoral votes for Kennedy.

1961

FEBRUARY 6

Students refused to pay fines and asked for jail sentences in Rock Hill. This was a "jail-in."

MARCH 2

Civil rights advocates staged an anti-segregation march on the state capitol in Columbia.

MAY 9

Civil Rights activists were attacked in Rock Hill when the Freedom Ride, which began on May 4, 1961, stopped in the city. The South Carolina portion of the trip witnessed the first instances of violent southern opposition.

MAY 15

The state launched its technical education program.

1962

MARCH 15

The General Assembly adopted a concurrent resolution requesting that the Confederate flag be "flown on the flagpole on top of the State House."

AUGUST 21

James Hinton ordered food at a Columbia Eckerd's and became the first African American to be served food at a formerly all-white lunch counter in South Carolina.

OCTOBER 24

Carolinas Virginia Nuclear Power Associated dedicated Parr Shoals (now V.C. Summer Nuclear Generating Station) in Fairfield County, the state's first nuclear power plant.

NOVEMBER 6

William D. Workman Jr.'s senatorial campaign against Olin D. Johnston ended in defeat but it demonstrated a new vitality in the South Carolina Republican Party.

1963

JANUARY 16

Gov. Donald S. Russell's inaugural barbecue was the first integrated public social event since Reconstruction.

JANUARY 28

Harvey Gantt became the first African American to enroll as a student at Clemson College.

SEPTEMBER 11

Robert G. Anderson, Henrie Montieth Treadwell, and James L. Solomon became the first African American students in the modern era to matriculate at the University of South Carolina.

1964

James McBride Dabbs' *Who Speaks for the South?* was published in New York.

JULY 2

The Federal Civil Rights Act, outlawing race, gender, religious, or ethnic-based discrimination in public accommodations and employment, became law.

SEPTEMBER 16

Senator Strom Thurmond left the Democratic Party and joined the Republican Party.

OCTOBER 29

Charles Townes of Greenville won the Nobel Prize in Physics.

NOVEMBER 3

Lyndon Johnson defeated Barry Goldwater for the presidency. Goldwater became the first Republican presidential candidate to carry South Carolina (eight electoral votes) since the end of Reconstruction.

VII

A Changing South Carolina
(1965–1999)

Integration in South Carolina was not a seamless process; there
were many bumps in the road and racially charged flash points in
the years following the passage of federal Civil Rights legislation.
Yet the legacy of the Civil Rights Movement in South Carolina was not
as fraught as in other Deep South states. African American political
power grew steadily through the end of the century. In 1965 African
Americans were neither in state or national offices representing South
Carolina nor judges sitting on high courts. By the turn of the century,
there were hundreds of African American elected officials in the state,
there was a powerful Legislative Black Caucus, James Clyburn was
the Majority Whip in the United States Congress, and Ernest Finney
wore the robes of the Chief Justice of the state's Supreme Court. Racial
divisions were closing, to be sure, but the waving of the Confederate
battle flag atop the State House beginning in 1962 and continuing to
fly until end of the century reminded anyone with eyes to see it that
some old wounds still festered and that there were fights remaining
ahead.

In the mid-1960s, South Carolinians began to abandon the Democratic Party. Although the state had been solidly Democratic since the
end of Reconstruction, the party of Civil Rights did not sit well with
many South Carolinians. Strom Thurmond had begun the exodus
to the Republican Party in the mid-1960s, many legislators switched
parties, and in 1974 the state elected its first Republican governor in
98 years. For the rest of the century, South Carolina's white voters, a
majority after 1920, increasingly supported Republican candidates for
local, state, and national offices.

A shift in the old legislative power structure was not unrelated. The battle over integration between county elites and metropolitan elites was just the most visible manifestation of a power struggle over who would control South Carolina. Federal courts mandated reapportionment of the General Assembly, which moved the state closer to the spirit of "one man, one vote," which also made it increasingly difficult, if not impossible for the old county delegation system of government to work. The metropolitan elites were the big winners in a shift to single member election districts and home rule for counties. These were also the politicians who championed statewide civic improvement in the final decades of the century. State leaders increasingly reached across a narrowing racial divide and supported initiatives that would benefit all segments of South Carolina society. Improving public education became more of a priority, as did reforming and streamlining state government.

Also during this period, South Carolina enjoyed great success in economic development. Policymakers developed an economic development strategy that attracted manufacturers to the state with a flexible workforce and a business-friendly government. Per capita income increased significantly and made great strides in approaching the national average. The state's population nearly grew by more than 50%, providing labor power to support rapid development.

1965

JANUARY 29

Joseph A. Vaughn enrolled at Furman University, which became the state's first private formerly all-white institution of higher education to integrate.

AUGUST 6

The Federal Voting Rights Act became law ending all barriers to African American voter registration.

1967

MARCH 1

An amendment to the state constitution opened the way for women to serve on juries in state courts.

MARCH 30

The General Assembly passed legislation that established the State Department of Parks, Recreation, and Tourism.

JUNE 20

The General Assembly passed legislation that established a "Brown Bag" law at the instance of the growing state tourism industry. One could carry a liquor bottle into a restaurant in a brown paper bag.

1968

The governor's office commissioned Moody's, a New York investment firm, to rate South Carolina's institutions and government. The report concluded that improvement in education should be the highest priority.

FEBRUARY 8

Three African American students at South Carolina State College in Orangeburg were shot and killed by Highway Patrol officers and 27 injured in the "Orangeburg Massacre." Students at the predominantly African American college had been protesting against the refusal of the white owner of a bowling alley to admit African American patrons.

MARCH 4

"Smokin' Joe" Frazier of Beaufort County defeated Jimmy Ellis to become the World Boxing Association's undisputed World Heavyweight Champion.

JULY

South Carolina's delegation to the turbulent Democratic National Convention at Chicago was integrated and as such was the only Southern state delegation that went unchallenged.

NOVEMBER 5

Richard Nixon defeated Hubert Humphrey and George Wallace for the presidency. South Carolina cast eight electoral votes for Nixon.

1969

FEBRUARY 25

Workers completed the 221-mile South Carolina portion of Interstate highway 26, linking the mountains to the coast.

MARCH 20

More than four hundred African American hospital workers, mostly female, went on strike against the all-white administration of the Medical College Hospital and Charleston County Hospital over unfair, racially differentiated pay and treatment by white hospital workers. The strike lasted until June 27, 1969.

NOVEMBER 21

The United States Senate rejected Clement Haynsworth's nomination to the US Supreme Court by President Nixon.

1970

US Census

White	1,794,430
African American	789,041
Native American	2,241
Filipino	1,222
Japanese	826
Chinese	521
Other	2,235
Total	2,590,516

Columbia became the first South Carolina city to exceed 100,000 in population.

MAY 7

Antiwar demonstrations at the University of South Carolina escalated into a takeover of the administration building, during which the National Guard was called to restore order.

JUNE 25

Gershwin's *Porgy and Bess* was performed in South Carolina for the first time. As part of the state's Tricentennial celebrations, fourteen performances were given before integrated audiences in the Charleston Municipal Auditorium.

NOVEMBER 3

Herbert U. Fielding, of Charleston, and James L. Felder and I. S. Leevy Johnson, of Columbia, won election as the first African American members of the South Carolina General Assembly since 1895.

1970–1971

Under federal court order, South Carolina desegregated its public schools.

1971

OCTOBER

The first integrated State Fair opened.

1972

Pat Conroy published *The Water is Wide* about his experience teaching on Daufuskie Island. This was the first of four of his novels to become a motion picture.

APRIL 20

Charles Duke, who grew up in Lancaster, became the tenth and youngest astronaut to walk on the moon as part of NASA's Apollo 16 mission.

NOVEMBER 7

The people of the state approved a constitutional amendment to revise the South Carolina judicial system.

NOVEMBER 7

Richard Nixon defeated George McGovern for reelection to the presidency. South Carolina cast eight electoral votes for Nixon.

1973

FEBRUARY 9

The state recorded its heaviest snowfall on record, from 24 inches in the central part of the state to 9 inches in Charleston.

FEBRUARY 11

Astronaut Col. Charles M. Duke Jr. became the first inductee of the South Carolina Hall of Fame at Myrtle Beach.

MARCH 29

South Carolina restaurants served the first legal mixed drinks in the state. The "brown bag" era was brought to a close by a constitutional amendment that was ratified by the legislature on March 28.

APRIL 4

The General Assembly passed legislation that implemented the constitutional provision for judicial reform.

JULY 6

Adjournment of the 100th General Assembly marked the last South Carolina legislature elected by counties. The United States Supreme Court had ruled June 25, 1973, in *Stevenson v. West*, that legislative districts coinciding with county or other political boundaries violated the principle of "one man, one vote." The state was reapportioned according to population.

1974

FEBRUARY 15

A corporate subsidiary of the Kuwait Sheikdom purchased Kiawah Island from C. C. Royal to develop as a resort.

APRIL 25

Riverbanks Zoo opened to the public. It became South Carolina's largest gated attraction, and would be recognized four times with the Southeastern Tourism Society's Shining Example Award as the Southeast's top tourist attraction.

JUNE 25

The Local Government Act provided counties more local control. However, since then, successive legislation has chipped away at the ability of local governments to deal with a variety of issues.

SEPTEMBER 23

Charles D. "Pug" Ravenel, the Democratic nominee for governor, was disqualified for not meeting the five-year residence requirement.

NOVEMBER 5

The election of Gov. James B. Edwards marked the rise of the modern Republican Party in the state and with it the return of the two-party system.

NOVEMBER 5

Juanita W. Goggins of York County became the first African American woman elected to the state legislature.

1975

The small number of African American state legislators formally organized the South Carolina Legislative Black Caucus.

JANUARY 31

The South Carolina Bar Association voted in favor of ending its existence. Members of that organization joined members of the State Bar to form the South Carolina Bar.

OCTOBER 13

The Patriot's Point Naval and Maritime Museum was dedicated in Mount Pleasant where the USS *Yorktown* is permanently anchored.

DECEMBER 9

Joseph P. Riley, Jr., won election as Mayor of Charleston.

1976

AUGUST 5

Thomas A. Yawkey, sportsman and conservationist, bequeathed 15,000 acres and $10 million to maintain a game preserve and wilderness area in Georgetown County.

OCTOBER 18

Congress enacted legislation to establish the Congaree Swamp National Monument. It would be designated a National Park in 2003.

NOVEMBER 2

Jimmy Carter defeated Gerald Ford for the presidency. South Carolina cast eight electoral votes for Ford.

1977

MAY

The first Spoleto Festival was held at Charleston.

JUNE 8

Gov. James B. Edwards signed the legislation that reestablished the death penalty.

JUNE 10

The General Assembly passed the Education Finance Act to establish an equitable basis for the distribution of public education funds.

SEPTEMBER 19

The United States Interior Department ruled that the Catawba Indians possessed a valid claim to 144,000 acres in York and Lancaster counties including the cities of Rock Hill and Fort Mill.

1978

NOVEMBER 7

Nancy Stevenson's election as Lieutenant Governor marked the first election of a woman to a statewide office.

Janie Glymph Goree of Carlisle became the first African American woman elected mayor in South Carolina.

1979

APRIL 23

Michelin Tire announced that it would build a $100 million plant in Lexington County, adding to its investment in the state that included facilities at Anderson, Greenville, and Spartanburg.

SEPTEMBER 22

Matthew J. Perry became the first African American federal judge in the history of South Carolina.

NOVEMBER 19

South Carolina native Lane Kirkland won election as president of the AFL-CIO.

1980

US Census

White	2,147,224
African American	948,623
Native American	5,665
Filipino	3,696
Asian Indian	2,152
Japanese	1,415
Chinese	1,404
Korean	1,390
Vietnamese	1,072
Hawaiian	439
Ghanaian	189
Samoan	77
Eskimo	70
Aleut	22
Other	8,382
Total	3,121,820

For the first time, the census reports showed a majority of South Carolinians (54.1%) lived in urban areas.

APRIL 19

The new Charleston Museum building opened.

JULY 8

Shawn Weatherly of Sumter was crowned "Miss Universe" in Seoul, South Korea.

OCTOBER 7

Congressman John Jenrette was convicted of accepting a $50,000 bribe from FBI agents masquerading as representatives of Arab sheiks seeking political favors.

OCTOBER 28

Gov. Richard Riley established the South Carolina Governor's School for the Arts through Executive Order in Greenville.

OCTOBER 28

The Catawbas brought suit against the state claiming title to 140,000 acres in Lancaster and York counties.

NOVEMBER 4

Ronald Reagan defeated Jimmy Carter for the presidency. South Carolina cast eight electoral votes for Reagan.

Lee Atwater gained national prominence as the mastermind of Ronald Reagan's "southern strategy." His campaign strategy through the election of 1988 made Atwater one of the leading figures in the national Republican Party.

DECEMBER 1

University of South Carolina football player George Rogers won the Heisman trophy.

NOVEMBER 2

US Customs officials made their first arrests in "Operation Jackpot" that uncovered international drug smuggling operations centered in South Carolina.

1982

APRIL

Reuben Greenberg was appointed Charleston's first African American Chief of Police.

JUNE 18

An agreement between a local environmental group that wished to protect the Santee Cooper basin and the Union Camp Corporation ended a year of negotiations. The paper mill was opened in Richland County in 1984.

1983

JANUARY

Filming of *The Big Chill* was completed in Beaufort. The movie opened in September and became the best-known production of the state's budding film industry.

FEBRUARY 2

South Carolina native Joseph Bernardin, the Archbishop of Chicago, was consecrated a Cardinal in the Catholic Church.

JULY 27

The General Assembly elected the members of the recently created six-judge Court of Appeals.

OCTOBER 25

The Reverend I. DeQuincy Newman won election as the first African American state senator in the twentieth century.

1984

JANUARY 1

The V. C. Summer nuclear reactor came online in Jenkinsville after thirteen years of delays from legal and civic opposition.

MARCH 28

Ten South Carolinians were killed when numerous tornadoes ravaged the state. Ronald Reagan declared four counties—Abbeville, Fairfield, Marlboro, and Newberry—disaster areas.

NOVEMBER 6

Richard Riley became the state's first governor elected to consecutive four-year terms.

NOVEMBER 6

Ronald Reagan defeated Walter Mondale for reelection to the presidency. South Carolina cast eight electoral votes for Reagan.

DECEMBER 31

The General Assembly passed the Education Improvement Act after Gov. Richard Riley convinced the legislature to increase the state sales tax by one cent to raise $250 million a year for public schools.

1985

JANUARY 16

Retired Chief Justice Joseph Moss, then serving as a special judge, was forced to leave the bench permanently after a furor over an alleged racial slur.

JULY 12

Ernest A. Finney Jr. became the first African American justice elected to the South Carolina Supreme Court since Reconstruction.

OCTOBER 14

Kingstree native Joseph L. Goldstein was awarded the Nobel Prize in medicine.

1986

Pat Conroy published his best-selling novel *The Prince of Tides*.

JANUARY 12

Astronaut Charles F. Bolden piloted the space shuttle Columbia in the 24th mission of NASA's Space Shuttle program.

JANUARY 22

Mack Trucks announced it would build an assembly plant in Fairfield County after South Carolina offered a $21 million incentive package. The plant would open August 3, 1987.

JANUARY 28

Astronaut Ronald E. McNair, a Lake City native, was killed in the Challenger explosion.

OCTOBER 27

The State-Record Company announced that it had been purchased by the Knight-Ridder Company, ending ninety-five years of local ownership.

NOVEMBER 4

Elizabeth Patterson became the first woman elected to the United States House of Representatives from South Carolina.

1987

MARCH 19

Jim Bakker, television evangelist, resigned and brought on the collapse of the PTL (Praise the Lord) religious empire centered in York County.

SEPTEMBER 11

Pope John Paul II visited Columbia.

1988

JANUARY 27

Jean Hoefer Toal became the first woman elected to the South Carolina Supreme Court.

APRIL 1

The *Columbia Record* ceased publication after ninety-one years.

JUNE 7

The General Assembly passed the Beachfront Management Act to control coastal development.

AUGUST 28

The Governor's School for Science and Mathematics opened to its first class on the campus of Coker College in Hartsville.

OCTOBER 7

Fuji Photo Film Co., Ltd., announced it would build its first US manufacturing facility in Greenwood.

OCTOBER 29

The State Museum opened in Columbia.

NOVEMBER 8

George Bush defeated Michael Dukakis for the presidency. South Carolina cast eight electoral votes for Bush.

1989

JANUARY 14

The Koger Center for the Arts opened in Columbia with a performance by the London Philharmonic Orchestra.

SEPTEMBER 21–22

Hurricane Hugo, a category 4 hurricane made landfall near Sullivan's Island. It brought a storm surge as high as nineteen feet above mean high tide and resulted in 35 deaths in South Carolina. Hugo left nearly 100,000 homeless and resulted in an estimated $7 billion

(1989 USD) in damages overall, making it the most damaging hurricane ever recorded at the time.

OCTOBER 11

FBI agents obtained the cooperation of lobbyist Ron Cobb and launched an investigation of corruption in the state legislature. Designated as Operation Lost Trust, the investigation resulted in numerous indictments and convictions over the next two years.

1990

US Census

White	2,406,974
African American	1,039,884
Native American	8,049
Eskimo	106
Aleut	91
Chinese	3,039
Filipino	5,521
Japanese	1,885
Asian Indian	3,900
Korean	2,577
Vietnamese	1,752
Cambodian	239
Hmong	76
Laotian	598
Thai	565
Other Asian	1,247
Hawaiian	426
Samoan	159
Guamanian	317
Other Pacific Islander	81
Other	9,217
Total	3,486,703

In the 1990 Census, 30,551 South Carolinians identified themselves as being of "Hispanic Origin."

Portions of the movie *Days of Thunder* were filmed at Darlington Raceway.

MAY 30

University of South Carolina President James B. Holderman resigned in the face of increasing criticism and controversy. He would
be indicted on criminal charges in March 1991.

JUNE 12

Democrats nominated Greenville Senator Theo Mitchell as their
candidate for governor, the first African American gubernatorial
nominee by a major party since Reconstruction.

JUNE 23

The first Gay and Lesbian Pride Parade marched down Main Street
in Columbia.

JULY 10

The Supreme Court of the United States awards South Carolina
13,000 acres of land in the lower reaches of the Savannah River,
resolving a decades-old border dispute with Georgia.

AUGUST 24

A Federal Grand Jury handed down the first indictments in the
Operation Lost Trust investigation.

SEPTEMBER 28

Charles P. Austin took the oath of office as Columbia's first African
American Chief of Police.

DECEMBER 1

The Peace Center for the Performing Arts opened in Greenville.

DECEMBER 2

Jazz musician and Cheraw native John Birks "Dizzy" Gillespie received the Kennedy Center Honors from President George H. W.
Bush.

1991

JANUARY 16

Operation Desert Storm began in the Middle East. Hundreds of
South Carolinians representing all branches of service participated
in the fighting.

DECEMBER 6

South Carolina National Bank, the state's oldest and largest bank,
merged with Wachovia Bank of Winston-Salem, North Carolina,
culminating a series of mergers and acquisitions that witnessed a
general consolidation of the state's banks.

1992

JANUARY 1

Sweeping new governmental ethics laws went into effect.

JANUARY 7

Voters approved the merger of the towns of Batesburg and Leesville.

JANUARY 16

Female lawmakers in the General Assembly formed the Women's Issues Caucus.

MAY 18

The South Carolina Baptist Convention voted to sever formal ties with Furman University.

JUNE 23

BMW (Bayerische Motoren Werke) announced that it would build its first automobile factory outside Germany in Greenville County.

AUGUST 30

The Catawba Indian Nation, after negotiations with state and federal officials, accepted $50 million in a preliminary agreement to settle their 152-year-old land dispute. The final settlement would become effective November 1993.

NOVEMBER 3

James Clyburn became the first African American elected to the United States Congress from South Carolina in the twentieth century. He would be elected co-president of his Congressional class.

NOVEMBER 3

Bill Clinton defeated George Bush for the presidency. South Carolina cast eight electoral votes for Bush.

NOVEMBER 3

Maggie Glover, of Florence County, became the first African American woman elected to the state senate.

DECEMBER 21

Former Gov. Richard Riley was selected by President-elect Bill Clinton to serve as Secretary of Education in the new administration.

1993

JANUARY 12

George Bush presented Strom Thurmond with the Presidential Medal of Freedom, the nation's highest civilian honor.

MARCH 31

The Myrtle Beach Air Force Base was closed.

JUNE 18

The General Assembly passed the Government Accountability and Reform Act which reorganized state government and gave the governor a cabinet of thirteen departments with the ability to hire and fire at will agency leaders at eleven of them.

SEPTEMBER 18

The First African American Miss South Carolina Kimberly Aiken of Columbia was crowned Miss America for 1994.

OCTOBER 13

Dreher High School (Columbia) graduate Kary Mullis was awarded the Nobel Prize for Chemistry.

OCTOBER 25

The National Football League chose Charlotte as one of its new expansion franchises. The Carolina Panthers, the Carolinas' first NFL team, played home games in their inaugural 1995 season at Clemson's Memorial Stadium.

OCTOBER 27

The Catawba Indian Nation was given federal recognition.

NOVEMBER 3

Spartanburg elected James Talley its first African American Mayor.

1994

Portions of the movie *Forrest Gump* were filmed in Beaufort, Colleton, and Hampton counties.

MAY 11

Hon. Ernest A. Finney Jr. won election as the first African American Chief Justice of the South Carolina Supreme Court since Reconstruction.

JULY 2

US Air Flight 1016, flying from Columbia to Charlotte, encountered heavy storm activity and crashed near the Charlotte airport.

Thirty-seven passengers died in the crash, at least 34 of whom were South Carolinians.

NOVEMBER 3

Authorities arrested Susan Smith for the murder of her young sons, 3 years and 14 months, by strapping them into their car seats and then letting her car roll into a lake in Union.

NOVEMBER 14

Republicans comprised the majority of the state House of Representatives for the first time since Reconstruction.

1995

MAY 27

"Cracked Rear View," the debut album of Columbia rock band Hootie and the Blowfish, reached #1 on the Billboard charts.

AUGUST 15

Shannon Faulkner became the first female to matriculate into the Citadel Corp of Cadets.

1996

MARCH 8

Strom Thurmond, at 93 years and 94 days old, became the oldest United States Senator in history.

APRIL 1

The Charleston Naval Base was closed.

MAY 21

South Carolina became the ninth state to ban same sex marriages.

AUGUST 17

Four Clarendon County members of the Ku Klux Klan were indicted for the burning of an immigrant migrant camp in February 1995 and two African American churches in June.

NOVEMBER 5

Bill Clinton defeated Bob Dole for reelection to the presidency. South Carolina cast eight electoral votes for Dole.

DECEMBER 1

Springs Industries closed its Olympia-Granby plant in Columbia. Olympia Mill had operated since 1899.

1997

JANUARY 19

Former United States Poet Laureate and bestselling author James Dickey died.

FEBRUARY 3

Former University of South Carolina standout and eight-time All Star Alex English was elected to the National Basketball Association Hall of Fame.

MAY 24

Strom Thurmond became the longest-serving United States Senator at 41 years, 9 months, and 31 days. He would serve until January 3, 2003.

JUNE 22

Myrtle Beach Aquarium opened.

AUGUST 26

Bridgestone/Firestone announced it would build a $435 million passenger and light truck tire manufacturing plant in Aiken County.

OCTOBER 7

George C. Rogers Jr., eminent South Carolina historian, died. Among the many books, articles, reviews, and essays he published in his career was the first edition of *A South Carolina Chronology*.

1998

MARCH 4

Camden native Larry Doby, the second African American player to break the Major League Baseball color barrier, was elected to the Hall of Fame by the Veterans Committee.

MARCH 17

Lake City native Darla Moore gave a $25 million gift to the Business School at her alma mater, the University of South Carolina. It was named the Darla Moore School of Business in her honor. She would donate another $45 million in matching funds to the school in 2004.

JUNE 20

Authorities seized one and a half tons of cocaine at the Port of Charleston with an estimated value of $100 million, the largest drug seizure in state history.

SEPTEMBER 3

The $63 million BI-LO Center (now Bon Secours Wellness Arena) opened in Greenville. It was the largest arena in the state until eclipsed by Columbia's Carolina Center in 2002.

OCTOBER 12

Charleston native Robert Furchgott won the 1998 Nobel Prize in medicine.

NOVEMBER 3

Voters eliminated the state's constitutional ban on interracial marriage which had been in effect since 1895.

NOVEMBER 17

James Clyburn won election as Chairman of the Congressional Black Caucus.

NOVEMBER 20

State officials agreed to a $2.2 billion settlement with four major tobacco companies that settled lawsuits by the state to recover costs associated with the treatment of smoking-related illnesses and restricted the advertising and marketing of tobacco products to young people.

1999

JUNE 2

Jean Hoefer Toal won election as the first female Chief Justice of the South Carolina Supreme Court.

OCTOBER 14

The South Carolina Supreme Court, in a unanimous ruling, prohibited the operation of video poker machines in the state. Payoffs would be outlawed after July 1, 2000.

OCTOBER 16

The National Board of the NAACP unanimously approved an economic boycott of South Carolina until the state stopped flying the Confederate flag from its State House grounds.

DECEMBER 4

The Strom Thurmond monument was dedicated on the State House grounds. A 2004 Joint Resolution of the General Assembly required it be modified to include the name of Essie Mae Washington among Thurmond's children.

Modern South Carolina
(2000–2020)

During the first decades of the 21st century, life and events in South Carolina closely reflected those of the nation. South Carolinians, horrified by the terrorist attacks in New York City and Washington, DC, reacted with displays of patriotism and a general acceptance of the reality that many personal freedoms would be limited in exchange for greater security. Personal screenings at airports and government buildings became the new normal.

The national "Great Recession," almost as disruptive but less permanent than the fear registered by terrorism, brought on a contraction in the state's economy from the end of 2007 through the remainder of the decade. Businesses failed and unemployment reached a generational high. South Carolina's economy shrank 6.4% during the recession, far greater than the national average. Terrorism and recession made this a decade of uncertainty.

The state remained overwhelmingly conservative politically and continued its transformation into a Republican party stronghold. By the end of the 2010s, all statewide officeholders and both houses of the General Assembly were Republican. As the first primary state, it became increasingly important in the selection of the party's nominee. Until the 2018 election, the state's representatives in Congress held key committee appointments. However, there was a changing of the old guard and signs of increasing diversity. The Democratic Party—in some ways—reflected national trends in that it exhibited strength in some urban areas—notably local offices in Charleston and Richland Counties. Strom Thurmond and Fritz Hollings, two of South

Carolina's longest serving US senators, retired. Nikki Haley became the first woman and non-white governor. The state's population grew at double-digit rates between 2000 and 2019, much faster than the rate of national increase—resulting in an additional congressional seat in 2010 and the possibility of another in 2020.

In the final years of the 2010s South Carolina exhibited even more of the characteristics of her sister states in the southeastern Sunbelt—politically and demographically. Again, mirroring national trends, the population of urban and coastal counties increased dramatically while that of rural counties declined. Seventeen counties lost population, and two (Allendale and McCormick) had fewer than 10,000 residents. Suburban counties—Berkeley and Dorchester (for Charleston) and York (Charlotte) had significant growth.

The city of Charleston became a cultural and economic magnet, assuming a major role in the state not seen in nearly two centuries. The main streets of small-town South Carolina became depressingly similar to those across the country—as populations declined and mom and pop businesses closed.

Despite the growth, education continued to be a significant problem. A television film, "The Corridor of Shame" made clear the difficulties facing poor, predominantly rural and African American school districts.

2000

US Census

White	2,695,560
Black or African American	1,185,216
American Indian and Alaskan Native	13,718
Asian Indian	8,356
Chinese	5,967
Filipino	6,423
Japanese	2,448
Korean	3,665
Vietnamese	4,248
Other Asian	4,907
Native Hawaiian	391
Guamanian or Chamorro	489

Samoan	277
Some other race	39,926
Two or more races	39,950
Total	4,012,012

In the 2000 Census, 95,076 South Carolinians identified themselves as "Hispanic or Latino."

Much of the movie *The Patriot* was filmed in several South Carolina locations.

MAY 19

The South Carolina Aquarium opened in Charleston.

JULY 1

The Confederate flag was removed from the State House dome. An historically accurate version of the battle flag was raised atop a flagpole at the Confederate monument on the grounds.

AUGUST 8

The wreckage of Confederate States of America submarine *H. L. Hunley* was raised near Charleston. The wreck had been discovered in 1970 and located in 1995. It was later put on display in North Charleston at the Warren Lasch Conservation Center.

NOVEMBER 8

Voters agreed to lift a ban on lotteries, clearing the way for the implementation of a state-run "Education Lottery." The General Assembly approved the establishment of a state lottery in June 2001, and the lottery began operating January 7, 2002.

DECEMBER 13

The Supreme Court of the United States, in *Bush v. Gore,* allowed Florida's earlier vote certification to stand, confirming George W. Bush's presidential electoral victory. South Carolina cast eight electoral votes for Bush.

2001

MARCH

Mack Trucks announced it was laying off 135 workers at its Winnsboro plant and a six-week shutdown in August.

MARCH 29

The African American History monument was dedicated, the first of its kind on any of the nation's statehouse grounds.

JUNE 13

The General Assembly passed the Education Lottery Act.

SEPTEMBER 11

Four coordinated Al Qaeda terrorist attacks killed nearly 3,000 Americans, setting in motion events that would significantly change many aspects of American life. In South Carolina, the immediate years following would witness an increased security presence, rising demands for veterans services, and increased defense spending in the state.

DECEMBER

Construction began on the $541 million Arthur Ravenel Bridge to replace the Cooper River Bridge connecting downtown Charleston to Mount Pleasant. It would open to traffic July 10, 2005.

2002

The Civil War movie *Cold Mountain* was filmed at South Carolina sites in Charleston and Berkeley counties.

APRIL 17

The Department of Energy notified South Carolina that shipments of plutonium to the Savannah River Site would begin in May.

JUNE 1

The University of South Carolina won the Women's Division I Outdoor Track & Field Championship.

NOVEMBER 5

Congressman Lindsey Graham won election to the United States Senate to replace retiring Strom Thurmond.

NOVEMBER 8

Volvo, which had purchased Mack Trucks in 2000, closed its Winnsboro plant and laid off its remaining 760 workers.

NOVEMBER 22

The University of South Carolina opened the Carolina Center, an 18,000-seat arena, the largest in the state of South Carolina and the eighth largest campus college arena.

2003

JANUARY 3

Strom Thurmond retired from the United States Senate after nearly 48 years and 16,348 votes.

MAY 30

Clemson University Men's golf team won the NCAA Division I Championship.

JUNE 26

Strom Thurmond died at 101.

AUGUST 22

John McKissick, Summerville High School football coach, recorded his 500th win, a national record. He went on to win 621 games by the time he retired in 2014.

2004

MAY 29

The USS *Pinckney*, the US Navy's 41st Arleigh Burke class guided-missile destroyer was commissioned. It was named for Beaufort native Petty Officer 1st Class William Pinckney, one of only four African Americans to earn the Navy Cross in World War II.

NOVEMBER 3

George W. Bush defeated John Kerry for reelection to the presidency. South Carolina cast eight electoral votes for Bush.

2005

The American Bible Society published *De Nyew Testament in Gullah Sea Island Creole,* a phonetic translation of the New Testament into the Gullah language.

JANUARY 3

Fritz Hollings retired from the United States Senate after 38 years.

JUNE 23

SCE&G officials dedicated the $275 million Lake Murray Dam backup project, constructed to mitigate a potential earthquake induced failure.

JULY 18

William Westmoreland, former commander of United States forces in Vietnam and Chief of Staff of the Army, died in Charleston.

2006

JANUARY 4

Congressman James Clyburn won election as Majority Whip, making him the number three-ranking leader in the United States House of Representatives.

NOVEMBER 7

South Carolina voters adopted a Constitutional amendment that defined marriage as the union between a man and a woman, thus, prohibiting recognition of same-sex marriage. A Federal court ruled this ban on same-sex marriage unconstitutional on November 12, 2014.

2007

JUNE 18

A fire at the Super Sofa store in Charleston claimed the lives of nine firefighters.

2008

JANUARY 26

Barack Obama won the state Democratic primary.

MAY 27

SCE&G and Santee-Cooper announced a contract with Westinghouse Electric to build a pressurized water reactor at the V.C. Summer Nuclear Generating Station. The $9 billion expansion project was abandoned in 2017.

NOVEMBER 4

Barack Obama defeated John McCain for the presidency. South Carolina cast eight electoral votes for McCain.

South Carolina's end of the year unemployment rate soared to a 25 year high of 8.4% as the state suffered with the rest of the nation in the "Great Recession." It would reach as high as 11.2% in 2010 and 2011.

2009

JUNE 18–24

Gov. Mark Sanford disappeared for a week. Supposedly hiking the Appalachian Trail, he was in fact in Argentina pursuing a romantic tryst. The General Assembly introduced an impeachment resolution that failed. However, he was censured for his deception.

SEPTEMBER 9

Congressman Addison Graves "Joe" Wilson, of South Carolina's second congressional district, shouted "You lie!" during an address by President Barack Obama to a joint session of Congress. The House of Representatives passed a "resolution of disapproval" against Wilson.

OCTOBER 28

The Boeing Company announced the selection of Charleston as the site for a $750 million assembly plant for the 787 Dreamliner.

2010

US Census

White	3,060,000
Black or African American	1,290,684
American Indian and Alaskan Native	19,524
Asian Indian	15,941
Chinese	9,686
Filipino	10,053
Japanese	2,413
Korean	4,876
Vietnamese	6,801
Other Asian	9,281
Native Hawaiian	570
Guamanian or Chamorro	1,046
Samoan	225
Other Pacific Islander	865
Some other race	113,464
Two or more races	79,935
Total	4,625, 364

In the 2010 Census, 235,682 South Carolinians identified themselves as "Hispanic or Latino."

JUNE 29

The University of South Carolina baseball team won the NCAA College World Series.

NOVEMBER 2

Nikki Haley won election as governor of South Carolina. A native of Bamberg and the daughter of Indian immigrants, she became the first woman and the first person of color to hold the office.

Tim Scott won election as the first African American Republican elected to Congress since Reconstruction.

Steve Benjamin won election as Columbia's first African American mayor.

2011

JUNE 28

The University of South Carolina baseball team won the NCAA College World Series for the second consecutive year, only the sixth school in history to do so.

As a result of the 2010 census, South Carolina received an additional congressional seat: The Seventh District

2012

APRIL 27

The first Dreamliner rolled off the assembly line at the Boeing plant in North Charleston.

NOVEMBER 6

Barack Obama defeated Mitt Romney for reelection to the presidency. South Carolina cast its nine electoral votes for Romney.

Mark Sanford won election to the United States House of Representatives, resurrecting his political career.

Tom Rice became the first person elected to represent the new Seventh Congressional District.

NOVEMBER 21

South Carolina native and entertainment legend James Brown was inducted into the Grammy Hall of Fame.

2013

JANUARY 2

Tim Scott was appointed United States Senator by Gov. Nikki Haley, replacing Senator Jim DeMint who had resigned. Scott became the first African American from South Carolina to serve in the US Senate.

JULY

Bravo television network filmed a new show, "Southern Charm," in Charleston. The series was still airing in 2020.

2014

OCTOBER 13

Bobby Harrell, Speaker of the South Carolina House of Representatives, pled guilty to state charges of misusing campaign monies and soon resigned from office.

NOVEMBER 4

Tim Scott won a special election to the United States Senate.

NOVEMBER 12

The South Carolina Supreme Court ruled in *Abbeville v. South Carolina* that the state had failed to do its duty to provide a "minimally adequate" education to children in the state's poorest school districts.

2015

APRIL 19

Charleston's *Post and Courier* won a Pulitzer Prize for public service for its series on domestic abuse: "'Till Death Us Do Part."

JUNE 17

During a Bible study, a white supremacist murdered nine African Americans at Emanuel A.M.E. Church in Charleston. The victims (now remembered as the Emanuel Nine) included the Rev. Clementa Pinckney, the church's pastor and a state senator.

JUNE 22

Thousands participated in an interracial Unity March on the Arthur Ravenel Bridge in Charleston, a visible outpouring of grief and community solidarity.

JUNE 26

The funeral of state Senator Clementa Pinckney was held in the TD Arena of the College of Charleston. President Barack Obama attended the service and delivered a stirring eulogy.

JULY 1

The newly created Department of Administration replaced the Budget and Control Board

JULY 9

After contentious debate in the General Assembly, Gov. Nikki Haley signed legislation calling for the removal of the Confederate battle flag from the State House Grounds.

JULY 10

The Confederate battle flag was removed from the State House grounds.

JULY 12

The NAACP ended its boycott of the state.

SEPTEMBER 8

Stephen Colbert, who grew up on James Island (and never fails to remind viewers of his home state), took over as host of CBS's "The Late Show."

OCTOBER 1–5

Torrential rains of historic proportions flooded much of the state. In the Columbia area, the rainfall and flooding were considered a 1,000-year event. Across the state there were nineteen fatalities, and eighteen dams collapsed or were breached.

2016

Travel + Leisure named Charleston the #1 tourist destination in the world—the first US destination to earn that honor.

JUNE 30

The Coastal Carolina University baseball team won the NCAA College World Series.

OCTOBER 8

Hurricane Matthew made landfall near McClellanville, bringing heavy rains and flooding to the northeastern portion of the state.

OCTOBER 21

Following Pat Conroy's death on March 4, the Pat Conroy Literary Center opened in Beaufort, coinciding with the first annual Pat Conroy Literary Festival.

NOVEMBER 8

Donald Trump defeated Hillary Clinton for the presidency. South Carolina cast its nine electoral votes for Trump.

2017

JANUARY 9

The Clemson Tigers won the NCAA football championship for 2016.

JANUARY 10

Dylan Roof was sentenced to death for the nine murders he committed at Emanuel A.M.E. Church in Charleston.

JANUARY 12

By Executive Order, President Barack Obama created the Reconstruction Era National Monument in Beaufort County.

JANUARY 24

Upon the resignation of Gov. Nikki Haley, Lt. Gov. Henry McMaster was sworn in as governor. He would be reelected in 2018.

JANUARY 25

Nikki Haley was sworn in as United States Ambassador to the United Nations.

APRIL 2

The Lady Gamecocks of the University of South Carolina won the NCAA women's basketball championship.

JULY 31

Santee-Cooper and South Carolina Electric & Gas announced that they would cease construction of two nuclear reactors at the V.C. Summer Nuclear Generating Station in Fairfield County.

NOVEMBER

Columbia-based Palmetto Health hospital system merged with Greenville Health System to create the largest not-for-profit hospital system in the state.

2018

MARCH 24

Navy destroyer USS *Ralph Johnson,* named for a Charleston native and Vietnam-era Medal of Honor recipient, was commissioned.

SEPTEMBER 14–15

Hurricane Florence, a category 1 storm, stalled off the coast causing heavy rainfall and flooding in the northeastern portion of the state. The town of Loris recorded 25.63 inches of rain.

SEPTEMBER 20

The rain-swollen Lumber and Little Pee Dee Rivers inundated the town of Nichols in Marion County for the second time in two years.

NOVEMBER 6

Joe Cunningham became the first Democrat elected to represent the First Congressional District since 1981.

JUNE 20

Volvo Car USA opened its first US plant in Ridgeville in Berkeley County. The $1.1 billion production plant will eventually employ 4,000 workers.

2019

JANUARY 2

The sale of SCANA Corporation (parent company of South Carolina Electric & Gas) to Dominion Energy was finalized.

JANUARY 8

The Clemson Tigers won their third NCAA championship in football. It was their second title in three years.

MARCH 12

By Act of Congress, two national monuments in the state became national historical parks. Fort Sumter National Monument became Fort Sumter and Fort Moultrie National Historical Park and the Reconstruction Era National Monument became the Reconstruction Era National Historical Park.

OCTOBER 15

The United States Supreme Court refused to hear South Carolina's appeal of a lower court decision that allowed the US Energy Department to stop construction of the Mixed Oxide Fuel Fabrication Facility at the Savannah River Site in Aiken County. The decision left unanswered the disposition of more than 20,000 pounds of radioactive plutonium stored at the site.

OCTOBER 25

Ground was broken for the International African American Museum in Charleston. The museum will be built on the site of Gadsden's wharf where tens of thousands of Africans were brought into the United States and into slavery.

2020

FEBRUARY 28

Joe Biden, with the endorsement of Jim Clyburn, wins the South Carolina Democratic state primary, setting up a likely November Joe Biden–Donald Trump presidential contest.

MARCH 16

The first COVID-19 virus death is recorded in South Carolina. The coronavirus global pandemic in 2020 forced the near-shutdown of South Carolina in April and resulted in economic disaster and unprecedented unemployment. According to the Centers for Disease Control and Prevention (CDC) there were more than 2,500 COVID-19 related deaths in the state (and >178,000 COVID-19 related deaths nationwide) as of August 27, 2020. At the time this work went to press, the full impact and consequences of the pandemic remained unknown.

MAY 30

Weeks of massive protests broke out in South Carolina in support of the Black Lives Matter movement, following the killing of George Floyd at the hands of Minnesota police officers. Several cities, including Charleston and Columbia, instituted curfews. Riots led to dozens of arrests.

Antiracist activism also led to the removal of or plans to remove statues, monuments, and memorials to the Confederacy and its leaders, outspoken racists, and colonialists. As of July, these removals included the John C. Calhoun monument in Charleston and the Confederate monument in Orangeburg; in addition, Clemson University's Calhoun Honors College has been renamed to Clemson University Honors College.

Abbeville, 87

Abbeville County, 50, 101, 106, 132

Abbeville v. South Carolina, 150

Abolitionists, 64, 72, 77, 84, 87

Acadians, 29

Active (ship), 34

Adams, John, 48, 55, 56

Adams, John Quincy, 66, 67

Adams, Mattie Jean, 98

AFL-CIO, 130

Africa/Africans: 2, British evacuate, 48;
  education, 27; imported as slaves, 9, 11,
  15, 25, 153; population, 9, 12, 15, 18, 21, 23,
  28, 36, 52, 57; revolts and conspiracies,
  23, 26, 54 ; in Yemassee War, 19

African American History monument, 145

African Americans: civil rights protests,
  121, 125; colleges and universities, 89, 90,
  94, 100; education, 71, 108, 119; elected
  to local and state offices, 90, 128, 130, 131,
  133, 149; elected to national office (post
  Reconstruction), 137, 149–50; integrate
  higher education, 100, 122, 124; labor
  strikes, 116, 126; mass murder of, 150,
  152; political activities, 89, 90, 102, 107,
  123, 130; population, 61, 63, 68, 73, 76,
  81, 90, 93, 96, 102, 104, 107, 110, 114, 118,
  120, 126, 130, 135, 143, 148; religion and
  religious leaders, 65, 85, 87; relocate to
  Liberia, 93; revolts and conspiracies, 65;
  segregation and suppression, 65, 80–81,
  88, 92, 94, 101, 107, 113, 116, 118, 124;
  service in Civil War, 84, 85

African Methodist Episcopal Church, 65,
  85

After the Storm, 115

Aiken, 89

Aiken County, 90, 91, 118, 140, 153

Aiken, Kimberly, 138

Al Qaeda, 145

Alabama, 53

Albemarle (ship), 8

Albemarle County, 13

Albemarle Point, 10, 11

Albemarle Sound, 1, 6, 9

Alcoholic beverages, 105, 112

Algonquian, 1, 3

Alien Act of 1784, 49

All Saints Parish, 34

Allen University, 94

Allen, Sara Campbell, 97

Allendale County, 107, 143

Altamaha River, 31

Alvin Theater, 112

American Bible Society, 146

American Colonization Society, 67

American Revolution, 21, 32–33, 38–48,
  49, 50

American Slavery As It Is, 72

Anderson (automobile), 105

Anderson County, 42, 130

Anderson District, 67

Anderson, John Gary

Anderson, Marian, 117

Anderson, Robert, 33

Anderson, Maj. Robert, 82, 86

Anderson, Robert G., 122

*Anecdotes of the Revolutionary War in
  America,* 64

Apalachees, 16

Apollo 16, 127
Appalachian Mountains, 1
Appalachian Trail, 147
Appomattox Courthouse, Virginia, 86
Arbuthnot, Marriot, 44, 45
Archaic Horizon Era, 2
Archdale, John, 14, 15
Argentina, 147
Army of Northern Virginia, 86
Arthur Ravenel Bridge, 145
Articles of Confederation, 43, 48, 50, 51
Ashley Grange No. 1, 91
Ashley River, 10, 12, 15, 48, 83
Asia, 1
Atlantic Ocean, 1
Atomic Energy Commission, 118
Atwater, Lee, 131
Audubon, John James, 69
Augusta, 55
Austin, Charles P., 136
Avery Normal Institute, 87
Avilés, Pedro Menéndez de, 5
Ayllon, Lucas Vasquez de, 3, 4,
Azor (ship), 93
Aztecs, 1

Bachman, John, 69
Bacon, Rebecca Pickens, 96
Bahama Islands, 3, 10, 22
Bakker, Jim, 134
Ball, John Coming, 46
Bamberg, 149
Bamberg County, 101
Bank of Charleston, 71
Bank of South Carolina, 58
Bank of the State of South Carolina, 61
Baptists, 13, 25, 74, 76, 77, 90
Barbados 6, 8, 9, 15, 43
Barnwell County, 50, 57, 90, 107, 118,
Barnwell, John, 18, 21
Bartram, John, 30
Baruch, Bernard, 103
Batesburg-Leesville, 137
Beachfront Management Act, 134
Beaufort: 13, 36, 61, 80, 84, 146, 151; Assembly called to meet at, 37; as capital 32;

early settlement; 10, 18; hurricane hits, 114, movie filmed in 132
Beaufort County, 93, 104, 125, 138, 152
Beauregard, Pierre G. T., 83
Beecher, Henry Ward, 86–87
Bell, John, 82
Bench and Bar, 79
Benedict College, 90
Benedict Institute. *See* Benedict College
Benedict, Bathsheba, 90
Benjamin, Steve, 149
Bennettsville, 95
Bering Sea, 1
Beringean land mass theory, 1
Berkeley County, 12, 35, 94, 143, 145, 153
Berkeley, John (Baron Berkeley of Stratton), 6
Berkeley, Sir William, 6
Bermuda, 10
Bernardin, Joseph, 132
Bethune, Mary McLeod, 112
Biden, Joe, 154
Bill of Rights, 52
BI-LO Center. *See* Bon Secours Wellness Arena
"Birth of a Nation," 105
Black Codes, 87, 88
Black Mingo Creek Bridge, 46
"Black Seventh" Congressional District, 94
Black Sox Scandal, 108
Blackbeard. *See* Thatch, Edward
Blackwood, Ibra C., 112
Blaine, James G., 94
Blanding, Abraham, 53
Blease, Coleman L ("Cole"), 81, 104, 111
Bluffton, 74
Bluffton Movement, 74
BMW (Bayerische Motoren Werke), 137
Boeing Company, 148, 149
Bolden, Charles F., 133
boll weevil, 99, 106, 107
Bon Secours Wellness Arena, 141
Bonnet, Stede, 20
Boone, Thomas, 31

Bowman v. Middleton, 55
Bowman, John, 51
Bravo television network, 150
Brayne, Henry, 11
Breckinridge, John C., 82
Bridgestone/Firestone, 140
Brisbane, William Henry, 84
Bristol, England, 3
British Museum, 22
Brookgreen Gardens, 111
Brooks, Preston, 78
Brown Fellowship Society, 52
Brown v. Board of Education of Topeka, 118, 119
Brown, Edgar, 119
Brown, James, 149
Bryan, William Jennings, 100, 102, 103
Budget and Control Board, 118, 151
Buford, Abraham, 45
Bull, William, II, 38
Bull, Stephen, 11
Bull, Brig. Gen. Stephen, 43
Bull, William, 30
Bulls Bay, 10, 17
Bureau of Refugees, Freedmen and Abandoned Lands, 86
Burke, Ædanus, 33
Burr, Aaron, 55, 58
Burt, Armistead, 87
Bush v. Gore, 144
Bush, George H. W., 134, 136, 137, 138
Bush, George W., 144, 146
Butler, Andrew, 78
Butler, Pierce, 51
Butler, Pierce M., 75
Byrnes, James F., 99, 111, 115, 116, 119

Cabot, John, 3
Calhoun County, 103
Calhoun, John Caldwell: 53, 61, 69, 95; defends slavery, 72; and nullification 69; as Secretary of State, 74; as Secretary of War, 63; as senator, 75, 76, 111; as Vice President, 66, 67, 70
Camden, 4, 36, 37, 47, 62, 66, 109, 140
Camden (Battle of), 45, 46

Camp (Fort) Jackson, 106, 114
Campbell, Archibald, 43
Campbell, William, 39, 40
Canby, E. R. S., 88, 89
Cape Fear, 9, 13, 14
Cape Fear River, 7
Cape Fear River (Battle of), 20
Cape Finisterre, Spain, 23
Capers, William, 68
Cardozo, Francis L., 87, 89
Carlisle, 130
Carolina (ship), 8, 10
"Carolina" (state song), 104
Carolina Center, 145
Carolina Panthers, 138
Carolina Public Service Authority, 112
Carolinas Virginia Nuclear Power Associated, 122
Carter, Jimmy, 129, 131
Carteret, George, 6
Cash, E. B. C., 93
Cash, Wilbur J., 114
Cass, Lewis, 75
Castle Pinckney, 55
Catawba River, 2–3,
Catawbas, 31, 73, 129, 131, 137, 138
Catesby, Mark, 22
Catholic Church, 55, 132
Catholics, 54, 64, 132
Cedar Springs, 73
Challenger (space shuttle), 133
Chamberlain, Daniel H., 91, 92
Charles City and Port. *See* Charleston
Charles I (King of England), 6
Charles II (King of England), 6
Charles IX (King of France), 5
Charles Town. *See* Charleston
Charles Town Library Society, 28, 38
Charlesfort, 5
Charleston: 5, 10, 13, 17, 24, 31, 33, 34, 36, 39; during American Revolution, 37, 38, 40, 41, 43, 44, 47; attempt to incorporate, 22; British evacuate, 48; epidemics in, 17, 25–26, 30, 71; established, 12; evolution of name, 32; falls to Federal troops, 80, 86; fires in, 15, 27, 42, 56, 71, 147;

Charleston (*continued*)
  free education established in, 19; hurricanes hit, 29, 114, 134; Loyalists in, 45, 46; mass murder in, 150, 152; pirates at, 9, 20; preservation in, 108, 111; Spoleto Festival, 129; tornadoes in, 114; as walled city, 16; Washington visits, 58
"The Charleston" (dance), 109
Charleston Bar, 75
Charleston City Council, 111
Charleston County Hospital, 126
Charleston Courier. See *Post and Courier*
Charleston earthquake of 1886, 95
Charleston hospital workers' strike of 1969, 126
Charleston Insurance Company, 56
Charleston Mechanic Society, 55
Charleston Municipal Auditorium, 126
Charleston Naval Base, 139
Charlestown Chamber of Commerce, 38
Charlestown Museum, 38, 42
Charlotte, North Carolina, 46, 138, 143
Cheraw, 36, 37, 66, 136
Cheraws, 19
Cherokee, 1, 32, 50; expeditions against, 30, 41; treaties with, 19, 23, 30, 31, 42, 62
Cherokee (ship), 40
Cherokee County, 101
Cherokee War, 30
Chesnut, Mary Boykin, 81
Chester County, 50,
Chesterfield County, 50
Cheves, Langdon, 62, 78
Chickasaws, 31
Chicora, 4
Chicorano, Francisco de, 3
child labor laws, 102–3 , 105, 106
Chiquola Mills, 112
Choctaws, 31
cholera, 71
Chowan County, 13
Christ Church Parish, 17
Church of England, 17, 26, 43
Churubusco (Battle of), 75
Circuit Court Act of 1768, 35
Circuit Court Act of 1769, 36

Citadel, 73, 82, 139
City Tavern, 49
Civil Rights Act of 1875, 91
Civil Right Acts of 1964, 100
Civil Right Acts of 1965, 100
Claflin University, 89
Clarendon County, 7, 118, 139,
Clarendon District, 77
Clay, Henry, 62, 66, 69, 74
Clemson College. *See* Clemson University
Clemson University, 95, 97, 99, 100, 122, 138, 146, 152, 153
Clemson, Thomas G., 95
Cleveland School, 109
Cleveland, Grover, 94, 95, 96, 97
Clinton, Bill, 137, 139
Clinton, DeWitt, 61
Clinton, Henry, 41, 44, 45
Clinton, Hillary, 151
Clovis culture, 2
Clyburn, James, 123, 137, 141, 147, 154
Coastal Carolina University, 151
Cobb, Ron, 135
Coker College, 134
Coker Pedigree Seed Company, 105
Coker, David R., 105, 106
Cokesbury, 87
Colbert, Stephen, 151
Cold Mountain, 145
College of Charleston, 49, 73, 107, 150
College World Series, 148, 149, 151
Colleton County, 12, 18, 48, 57,
Colleton, James, 14
Colleton, John, 6
Columbia: 51, 64, 67, 71, 75, 90, 91, 96, 105, 109, 138; African American Convention, 107; 52; airport, 110; army camp, 106; as capital 33, 52; chief of police, 136: civil rights march, 121; falls to Federal troops and burned , 86; Federal troops withdrawn (1877), 92; first gay and lesbian pride parade, 136; first television station, 119; founding, 50, 51; General Hospital opened, 101; Lafayette visits, 66; mayor, 149; nullification, 69; Olympia Mills, 98, 139; Pope John Paul II visits, 134;

population, 88, 126; railroad transportation from, 73, 77; Sherman and, 80; Secession Convention, 82; State Fair, 78; state offices in, 66, 87; State Penitentiary, 88, 113; Washington visits, 55

Columbia (space shuttle), 133

Columbia Army Air Base, 115

Columbia Canal, 66

Columbia College, 79

Columbia Female College. *See* Columbia College

Columbia Mills Company, 97

Columbia Museum of Art, 118

Columbia Record, 134

Combahee Bluff, 48

Combahee River, 84

Commission on Civic Preparedness for War, 106

Commons House of Assembly: 21, 28, 34; act of, concerning pirates, 20; asserts authority, 22, 29, 31, 34; on education, 19; enacts election law, 21; enacts fire code, 15; establishes religion, 17; issues paper money, 16; and Proprietary rule, 20; and trade with Native Americans, 18

Compromise of 1808, 60

Compromise of 1850, 76

Conception (ship), 27

Concessions and Agreements, 7

Concord, Massachusetts, 39

Confederate flag, 121, 123, 141, 144, 151

Confederate States of America, 80, 83, 144

Confitachiqui, 2, 4

Congaree Fort, 20

Congaree River, 47, 50, 88

Congaree River (Gervais Street) Bridge, 109

Congaree Swamp National Park, 129

Congregation Beth Elohim, 28, 55

Congregationalists, 12

Congressional Black Caucus, 123, 141

Conner, James, 82

Continental Association, 39

Converse College, 95

Converse Manufacturing Company, 88

Converse, Dexter E., 88

Conyers, John Henry, 91

Coolidge, Calvin, 109

Cooper River, 12, 13, 15, 50, 83

Cooper River Bridge, 110, 145

Cooper, Anthony Ashley (Baron Ashley of Wimborne St. Giles), 6, 7

Cooper, Thomas, 64, 67, 71

Cooperationists, 77, 78

Cork, Ireland, 64

Cornell Arms building, 117

Cornwallis, Charles, 45, 46, 47

Coronavirus. *See* COVID-19

"The Corridor of Shame," 143

cotton: 10, 53, 58; Sea Island, 52, 107; short staple (upland), 55, 63, 69

cotton gin, 55, 58

County Court Act of 1785, 49–50

county delegation system, 124

Coventry, Rhode Island, 62

COVID-19, 154

Cowpens (Battle of), 46

Cox, James M., 108

Craven County, 12, 35

Craven, William (Earl of Craven), 6

Crawford, William, 66

Creeks, 19, 20, 31

"The Crime Against Kansas," 78

Crisp, Edward, 16

Crokatt, James, 29

crop-lien system, 88

Crum, William D., 102

Cuming, Alexander, 23

Cunningham, Ann Pamela, 78

Cunningham, Joe, 153

Currituck County, 13

Cusabo, 2

Dabbs, James McBride, 122

Dan River, 47

Darla Moore School of Business, 140

Darlington County, 50, 95, 101

Darlington Raceway, 118, 135

Darlington Riot, 97

David (Confederate submarine), 85

Davis, Jefferson, 87

Davis, John W., 109

Days of Thunder, 135
De Nyew Testament in Gullah Sea Island Creole, 146
death penalty, 129
Debs, Eugene V., 104
Declaration of Independence, 37, 41
Declaratory Act, 34
Defence (ship), 40
DeMint, Jim, 149
Democratic Party, 81, 116, 117, 119, 122, 123, 128, 142
Denmark, 100
Department of Administration, 151
Department of Energy, 145, 153
Dewey, Thomas E., 116, 117
Dibble Plan, 94
Dickey, James, 140
Dillon County, 104
Dills Bluff, 48
Dispensary, 97, 103
Dixiecrats, 117
Doby, Larry, 140
Dock Street Theatre, 113
Dole, Bob, 149
Dominion Energy, 153
Doolittle, Jimmy, 115
Dorchester (town in Massachusetts), 15
Dorchester (town in South Carolina), 48
Dorchester County, 101, 143
Douglas, Stephen, 82
Drayton, William Henry, 40, 41, 42, 43
Dreher High School, 120, 138
Dreher Shoals Dam, 110, 111
dueling, 93
Dukakis, Michael, 134
Duke Power Company, 111
Duke, Charles, 127
Dupont Corporation, 118
DuPont, Gideon, 49
DuPont, Samuel Francis, 84

Earle, Willie, 117
Ebenezer, Georgia, 27
Eckerd's drugstore, 121
Edgefield County, 50, 100, 101, 106,
Edgefield Pottery, 62

Edict of Nantes, 13
Edisto Island, 114
Edisto River, 6, 48
Education Finance Act, 129
Education Improvement Act, 132
Education Lottery Act, 144, 145
Edwards, James B., 128, 129
Ehrhardt, 89
Eight Box Voting law, 94
Eighteenth Amendment , 111
Eisenhower, Dwight, 119, 120
Elkison v. Deliesseline, 65
Ellenton Riot, 91
Elliott, Robert B., 91
Elliott, William, 52
Ellis, Jimmy, 125
Ellis, Mary Gordon, 109
Elmore v. Rice, 117
Emancipation Proclamation, 84
Emanuel A.M.E. Church, 65, 150, 152
Emanuel Nine, 150
Embargo Act, 60
England, John, 64
English Bill of Rights, 14
English, Alex, 140
enslaved people: African, 2, 9, 32, 39, 59; active in Civil War, 84, 85; freed, 83; legislation concerning, 26, 34, 71; Native American, 3, 16, 18; population, 9, 12, 15, 18, 23, 28, 52, 57, 61, 63, 68, 73, 76, 81 revolts and conspiracies, 4, 23, 26, 54, 62, 77
Episcopal Calvary Church, 75
Episcopal Church, 56
Erskine College, 72
Eutaw Springs (Battle of), 47, 48
Evans, Matilda Arabelle, 101
Eve, Abraham, 55
Exposition and Protest, 68

Fairfield County, 1, 50, 122, 132, 152
Falmouth, England, 31
Faulkner, Shannon, 139
Fayetteville, North Carolina 66
Federalist Party, 59, 60
Felder, James L., 126

Fence Law, 92
Ferguson, Patrick, 44, 46
Fielding, Herbert U., 126
54th Massachusetts Regiment, 85
Fillmore, Millard, 78
Finley, David Edward, 115, 118
Finney, Ernest, 123, 133, 138
Fireproof Building, 65
Fires, 15, 27, 42, 56, 71, 147
First Bank of the United States, 55,
First Continental Congress, 38
First Regiment of South Carolina Volun-
    teers, 84
Fishdam Ford, 46
Fishing Creek, 45
Fleming, C.E., 94
floods, 103, 106, 151, 152
"Flora, or Hob in the Well" (opera), 25
Florence County, 95, 137
Florida, 3, 4, 5, 6, 7, 144
Floyd, John, 69
football, 95, 100, 131, 138, 146, 152, 153
Force Bill, 70
Ford, Gerald, 129
Forrest Gump, 138
Fort Caroline, 5
Fort Charlotte, 39
Fort Granby, 47
Fort Jackson, 106, 114
Fort Mechanic, 55–56
Fort Motte, 47
Fort Moultrie, 41, 44, 67, 82, 153
Fort Moultrie (Battle of), 41, 42
Fort San Felipe, 5, 6
Fort San Marcos, 6
Fort Sumter, 83, 85,
Fort Sumter (Battle of), 85
Fort Sumter and Fort Moultrie National
    Historical Park, 153
Fort Sumter National Monument. See Fort
    Sumter and Fort Moultrie National
    Historical Park
Fort Wagner, 85
Fort Watson, 47
Fourteenth Amendment, 88, 89
Fox, George, 12

France/French: 54, 55, 105; and American
    Revolution, 42, 45; early exploration
    and settlement, 2, 4, 5, 12; Edict of
    Nantes, 13; Revolution, 53; war with, 16,
    17, 27, 29; XYZ Affair, 56, 57
Franklin, Benjamin, 48
Frazier, "Smokin' Joe," 125
Freedmen's Bureau. See Bureau of Refu-
    gees, Freedmen and Abandoned Lands
Freedom Rides, 121
Frémont, John C., 78
French and Indian War, 29, 31, 32
French Broad River, 4
French Revolution, 53
Friday's Ferry, 50
Friendly Society for the Mutual Insuring
    of Houses against Fire, 25, 27
Friendship Junior College, 121
Frogmore, 84
Fundamental Constitutions of Carolina,
    7–8, 10, 12, 14, 15
Furchgott, Robert, 141
Furman University, 76, 77, 95, 124, 137

Gadsden, Christopher, 31, 33, 34, 38, 40,
    46, 48, 59
Gadsden's wharf, 153
gag rule, 71
Gage, Thomas, 39
Gaillard, John, 59
Gantt, Harvey, 100, 122
Garden, Alexander, 27, 30, 64
Garfield, James A., 93
Garrison, William Lloyd, 87
Gary, Martin W., 86, 87
Gates, Horatio, 45
Gay and Lesbian Pride Parade, 136
General Assembly: African American
    members, 126; alcoholic beverages,
    103, 112, 125; American Revolution,
    42, 48, 52; apportionment, 124, 128;
    banks, 58, 61, 71; capital moved to Co-
    lumbia, 50, 52; chartering corporations,
    97; Confederate flag, 121, 151; Consti-
    tution ratified, 51; courts and judicial
    reform, 36, 58, 89, 127, 132;

General Assembly (*continued*)
  creating counties/districts, 50, 54, 57, 58,
  67, 77, 89, 90, 93, 94, 95, 100, 101, 102, 103,
  104, 106, 107; divorce, 117; education,
  61, 64, 71, 90, 92, 103, 105, 109, 129, 132;
  elections, 94, 116; environmental laws,
  134; established penitentiary, 88; establishing colleges/universities, 49, 69,
  76, 78, 89, 90, 94, 100; establishing state
  boards, commissions, and departments,
  50, 67, 88, 93, 104, 105, 106, 109, 110, 113,
  115, 125; governmental accountability,
  138; impeachment of Sanford, 147–48;
  incorporated Charleston, 49; incorporation of religious bodies, 55; labor, 102,
  108, 119; lottery, 144, 145; Massachusetts
  Circular Letter considered, 35; military/
  militia, 65, 73; monuments, 141; Negro
  Seamen's Acts, 65, 66; paper money
  issued, 50; public executions, 93; public
  utilities, 57; race relations, 65, 92, 101,
  120; slavery, 51, 58, 59; social security,
  113; state flower, 109; state song, 104;
  state tree, 114; taxation, 101; transporta-
  tion, 67; women's issues, 106, 137
General Hospital, 101
General School Act of 1871, 90
General Synod of the Associate Reformed
  Presbyterian Church, 72
Genêt, Edmond-Charles, 55
George II (King of England), 23, 29
George III (King of England), 32, 36, 42
George Town. *See* Georgetown
Georgetown, 10, 23, 29, 36, 37, 47, 55, 58, 65,
  86, 97, 102, 111
Georgetown County, 68, 129
Georgia, 7, 24, 27, 31, 42, 43, 46, 136
German Colonization Society of Charles-
  ton, 75
Germans, 24, 25, 75
Germany, 105, 107, 114, 137
Gershwin, George, 112, 126
Gershwin, Ira, 112, 126
Gibbes Art Gallery, 103
Gibbes, Frances Guignard, 98
Gibbes, James S., 103

Gibson, Althea, 120
Gillespie, John Birks "Dizzy," 136
Gillmore, Quincy A., 87
Gillon, Alexander, 43, 45
Gilman, Caroline, 69
Glen, James, 27
"Glorious Revolution," 13
Glover, Maggie, 137,
Godbold, Lucile Ellerbe, 108
Goggins, Juanita W., 128
Goldstein, Joseph L., 133
Goldwater, Barry, 122
Gonzales, N. G., 96, 102
Goose Creek, 57
Gordillo, Francisco, 3
Gore, Al, 144
Goree, Janie Glymph, 130
Government Accountability and Reform
  Act, 138
Governor's Mansion, 88
Governor's School for Science and Mathe-
  matics, 134
Graham, Lindsey, 145
Grammy Hall of Fame, 149
Grange, 90, 95
Graniteville Manufacturing Company, 74
Grant, James, 30
Grant, Ulysses S., 86, 89, 91, 92
Granville County, 18, 19
Gray, Wil Lou, 108
Grayson, William, 54, 77
"Great Recession," 142, 147
Great Seal of the Royal Province, 40
Great Seal of the State, 41, 66
Great War for the Empire. *See* French and
  Indian War
Greely, Horace, 91
Greenberg, Reuben, 131
Greene, Nathaniel, 33, 46, 47, 48
Greenville Baptist Female College, 77
Greenville County, 50, 137
Greenville Health System, 152
Greenville Symphony, 117
Greenwood County, 101, 103, 106
Gregg, William, 74
Grenville Packet (ship), 31

Grimké, Angelina, 64, 72
Grimké, John F., 64
Grimké, Sarah, 64, 72
Guerard, Peter Jacob, 14
Guignard, Gabriel, 51
Guilford Courthouse (Battle of), 47
Gullah language, 146

Haley, Nikki, 143, 149, 151, 152
Hamburg, 70, 91
Hamburg Riot, 91
Hamilton, James, 70
Hampton County, 93, 104, 107, 138
Hampton, Wade, 33
Hampton, Wade, III, 81, 85, 92, 93, 96
Hancock, John, 52
Hancock, Winfield Scott, 93
Hanging Rock, 45
Harding, Warren G., 108
Harleston, Edwin A., 106
Harleston's Green, 51
Harper, Robert Goodloe, 56
Harper, William, 70, 72
Harrell, Bobby, 150
Harrington, James, 7
Harrison, Benjamin, 95, 96
Harrison, William H., 73
Hart, Oliver, 40
Hartsville, 101, 134
Hawker, James, 34
Hayes, Rutherford B., 92
Hayne, Henry E., 91
Hayne, Isaac, 47
Hayne, Robert Y., 67, 68, 70,
Haynsworth, Clement, 126
Heath, Robert, 6
Heisman trophy, 131
Heyward, DuBose, 112
Heyward, Duncan Clinch, 81
Heyward, Thomas, 41, 43
Hibernian Society, 58
Higginson, Thomas W., 84
Highland Park Hotel, 89
Highway Patrol, 110, 125
Hill, William, 45
Hilton Head Island, 7, 52, 61, 83, 84,

Hilton, William, 6
Hinton, James, 121
"The Hireling and the Slave," 77
Hispaniola, 3
Hoar, Samuel, 74
Hobcaw, 39
Hobcaw Barony, 103
Hobkirk's Hill, 47
Holderman, James B., 136
Holland, 46
Hollings, Ernest "Fritz," 142, 146
Honea Path, 112
hookworm, 99
Hootie and the Blowfish, 139
Hoover, Herbert, 110, 111
Horlbeck, John Adam, 34
Horlbeck, Peter, 34
Horry District, 58
Housatonic (ship), 85
Huck, Christian, 45
Huger, Benjamin, 42
Huger, Isaac, 44
Huguenots, 5, 12, 13, 28
Humphrey, Hubert, 125
Hunley (Confederate submarine), 85, 144
Huntington, Anna Vaughan Hyatt, 111
Huntington, Archer Milton, 111
Hurricanes: 99; 1752, 29; 1813, 61; 1820, 65;
    1822, 65; 1893, 97; 1911, 104; 1940, 114;
    Florence, 152; Hugo, 134–135; Matthew,
    151
Hutson, Richard, 43
Hyde, Edward (Earl of Clarendon), 6, 18

"I'll Overcome Some Day," 116
Incas, 1
Independent Church, 12
Indians. See Native Americans
Indien (ship). See South Carolina (ship)
indigo, 10, 27, 28, 29, 50
Industrial Workers of the World, 105
influenza, 107
Institute Hall, 82
International African American Museum,
    153
Interstate and West Indian Exposition, 102

Irby, John L. M., 96
Irish, 12, 58
Iroquois, 1, 3
Isle of Palms, 41

Jackson, Andrew, 66, 67, 68, 69, 106
Jackson, "Shoeless" Joe, 108
Jacksonborough, 45, 46, 48
jail-ins, 121
James II (King of England), 13
James Island, 48, 84, 151
Jasper County, 104, 109
Jasper, William, 41, 44
Jay, John, 48
Jefferson, Thomas, 56, 58, 59, 68
Jenkinsville, 132
Jenrette, John, 131
Jeremiah, Thomas "Jerry," 40
Jews, 15, 28, 55, 66
John Adams (ship), 57
Johns Island, 44
Johns, Jasper, 120
Johnson, Andrew, 87
Johnson, David, 70
Johnson, Henrietta Dering, 17
Johnson, I. S. Leevy, 126
Johnson, Lyndon, 122
Johnson, Nathaniel, 17, 18, 23
Johnson, Olin D., 112, 113, 116, 122
Johnson, Robert, 21, 23, 24
Johnson, William, 59, 65

Kahal Kadosh Beth Elohim. *See* Congre-
    gation Beth Elohim
Kalb, Baron de, 42, 45
Kennedy Center Honors, 136
Kennedy, John F., 121
Kerry, John, 146
Kershaw County, 3, 54, 102
Kettle Creek (Battle of), 43
Kiawah Island, 128
Kiawah, Cacique of, 2, 10
King George's War, 27
King, Rufus, 62
King's Mountain (Battle of), 46
Kinsale, Ireland, 8

Kirkland, Lane, 130
Knight-Ridder Company, 133
Koger Center for the Arts, 134
Ku Klux Klan, 139
Ku Klux Klan Act, 91
kudzu, 112
Kuwait, 128

La Florida (*see* Florida)
Lafayette, Marquis de, 42, 66
LaFollette, Robert M., 109
Lake City, 133, 140
Lake Marion, 115
Lake Moultrie, 115
Lake Murray, 110, 146
Lancaster County, 50, 127, 129, 131
Lander Academy. *See* Lander College
Lander College, 103
Landis, Judge Kenesaw Mountain, 108
Landon, Alf, 113
"The Late Show," 151
Laudonnière, Rene de, 5
Laurens County, 50, 78
Laurens, Henry, 39, 41, 42, 43, 46, 48
Laurens, John, 48
Laws of the Province of South-Carolina,
    The, 25
Lee County, 102
Lee, Arthur, 39
Lee, Harry (Light Horse), 47
Lee, Robert E., 86
Legare, James M., 53
Lewisburg County. *See* Lexington County
Lexington and Concord (Battle of), 39
Lexington County, 25, 50, 90, 102, 103, 111,
    130
Lieber, Francis, 71
Lincoln, Abraham, 82, 83, 87
Lincoln, Benjamin, 44
Lining, John, 25
Little Pee Dee River, 153
Little River, 55
Liverpool, England, 63
Local Government Act, 128
Locke, John, 7
London Philharmonic Orchestra, 134

London, England, 20, 23, 29, 32, 39, 46
Long Island. *See* Isle of Palms
Lords Proprietors, 6, 7, 11, 12, 14, 18, 23
Loris, 152
lottery, 144, 145
Louis XIV (King of France), 13
Louisiana, 53
Lowndes, Rawlins, 42
Lowndes, William, 61
Lucas, Jonathan, 51
Ludwell, Phillip, 14
Lumber River, 153
Lutheran Church, 27,78
Luxembourg, Chevalier de, 45
Lynch, Thomas, 33, 38
Lynch, Thomas, Jr., 41
Lyttelton, William Henry, 30

Mack Trucks, 133, 144, 145
Madagascar, 11
Madison, James, 60, 61
Magrath, Andrew Gordon, 72, 85
Maham, Hezekiah, 47
Major League Baseball, 108, 140
Major League Baseball Hall of Fame, 140
malaria, 9, 99
Mangum, Willie P., 72
Manning, Richard I., 81, 105, 106
Margravate of Azilia, 20
Marion, Francis, 33, 46, 47
Marlboro County, 50, 132
Mars Bluff, 35
Marshall, J. Q., 102
Marshall, John, 56
Martyr, Peter, 4
Mason, James Murray, 76, 83
Massachusetts, 13, 15, 35, 39, 74, 78, 84, 85
Massachusetts Circular Letter, 35
Mathews, John, 43, 48
Maxwell, Cassandra, 115
May chemical plant, 118
Mayans, 1
Maybank, Burnet, 114
Mayesville, 112
McCain, John, 147
McClellanville, 151

McCord, David J., 71
McCormick County, 106, 143
McCrady, Edward, 101
McDuffie, George, 69
McGovern, George, 127
McKinley, William, 100, 102
McKissick, John, 146
McKnight, Marian, 120
McLaurin, John L., 102
McMaster, Henry, 152
McNair, Ronald E., 133
Medal of Honor, 107, 152
Medical College Hospital, 126
Medical College of the State of South
    Carolina, 69
Medical Society of South Carolina, 56
Meeting Street (Charleston), 12, 29, 37,
    40, 57
Memoir on Slavery, 72
Mexican War, 74, 75
Mexico, 66, 74, 75
Miami, Florida, 117
Michelin Tire, 130
Middleburg, 115
Middleton, Arthur, 41
Middleton, Henry, 38
Middleton, Thomas, 30
Miller, Phineas, 58
Miller, Thomas E., 98, 100
Mills, Robert, 53, 64, 65, 73
Mind of the South, The, 114
Miss America, 120, 138
Miss South Carolina, 138
Miss Universe, 131
Mississippi, 53
Mitchel, Ormsby, 84
Mitchell, Theo, 136
Mitchelville, 84
Moderators, 36
Monaghan Mill, 105
Monck, George (Duke of Albemarle), 6
Moncks Corner, 44
Mondale, Walter, 132
Montague, Charles, 37
Montgomery, Alabama, 83
Montgomery, John H., 94

Montgomery, Robert, 20
Moody's, 125
Moore, Darla, 140
Moore, James, 16
Moore, James (the younger), 19, 21
Moore, Sallie Flournoy, 93
Morgan, Daniel, 46
Morris Island, 82, 85
Moss, Joseph, 133
Motte, Rebecca, 47
Moultrie, William, 41,43, 44, 49
Mount Dearborn Armory, 58
Mount Pleasant, 110, 129, 145
Mt. Vernon Ladies Association, 78
Muhlenberg, Heinrich Melchior, 27
Mulberry Mound, 3
Mullis, Kary, 138
Murray, Ellen, 84
Murray, George Washington, 87
Muschamp, George, 13
Muskogean, 1,3
Mutual Insurance Company, 56
Myrtle Beach, 4, 109, 127, 138, 140
Myrtle Beach Air Force Base, 138
Myrtle Beach Aquarium, 140

Nairne, Thomas, 17
NASA, 127, 133
NASCAR, 118
Nashville, Tennessee, 76
Nation Ford Treaty, 73
National Association for the Advance-
    ment of Colored People (NAACP),
    106, 108, 118, 141, 151
National Basketball Association, 140
National Football League, 138
National Gallery of Art, 115
National Guard, 106, 112, 126
National Trust for Historic Preservation,
    118
National Youth Administration, 112
Native Americans: 2, 9, 10, 17, 19, 31, 39,
    62, 72, 73, 129, 137, 138; enslaved, 11, 18;
    population, 18, 120, 126, 130, 135, 143, 148;
    trade, 9, 11, 18; war with Europeans, 6,
    18, 29

naval stores, 10, 18
Navigation Acts, 13
Navy Cross, 146
Negro Act of 1740, 26
Negro Seamen's Act, 65, 66
Nelson, Annie Greene, 115
New Acquisition District, 45
New Deal, 115
New England, 15, 16, 94
New England Society, 75
New Ironsides (ship), 85
New Jersey, 50
New York, 30, 33, 45, 71, 78, 94, 110, 112, 120,
    122, 125, 142
New York Stock Exchange, 110
Newberry College, 78
Newberry County, 50, 132
Newcastle, Pennsylvania, 25
Newfoundland, 3, 46
Newman, I. DeQuincy, 132
Niagara (ship), 83
Nichols, 153
Nicholson, Francis, 21
Niernsee, John R., 77
Nineteenth Amendment, 108
Ninety Six, 36, 37, 40, 47, 49
Nixon, Richard, 121, 125, 126, 127
Nobel Prize, 122, 138, 141
North Carolina: 9, 14, 18, 19, 31, 66, 72, 86,
    88, 106, 136; border, 7, 25; in the Ameri-
    can Revolution, 43, 46, 47
North Island, 42, 65
Nova Scotia, 29
nullification, 69, 70

O'Neall, John Belton, 70, 75, 79
Obama, Barack, 147, 148, 149, 150, 152
Ocean Forest Hotel, 109
Oconee County, 42, 89
Oconostota, 30
Office of Economic Stabilization, 115
Office of War Mobilization, 115
Oglethorpe, James, 24
Ohio River, 54
Olympia Mill, 98, 139
Olympics, 108

Operation Desert Storm, 136
Operation Jackpot, 131
Operation Lost Trust, 135, 136
Opportunity School, 108
Orange Parish, 43
Orangeburg, 24, 36, 37, 47, 89, 90, 100, 103, 115
Orangeburg Massacre, 125
Ordinance of Nullification, 69, 70
Ordinance of Secession, 82
Orr, James L., 78, 87, 89
Osceola, 72
Osteneco, 30
Over-the-mountain men, 46
Owens Field airport, 110
Oyster Point, 11, 12

Pacolet Manufacturing Company, 94
Pacolet River, 38, 103
Paine, Thomas, 40
Palmer, John, 23
Palmetto Day, 42
Palmetto Health, 152
Palmetto Regiment, 74, 75
palmetto tree, 41
Pardo, Juan, 5
Parker, Alton B., 103
Parker, Lewis, 105
Parker, Peter, 41
Parliament, 14, 17, 23, 28, 33, 34, 36
Parr Shoals (see V.C. Summer Nuclear Generating Station)
Parris Island, 5, 96
Pasquotank County, 13
Pat Conroy, 127, 133, 151
Pat Conroy Literary Center, 151
Pat Conroy Literary Festival, 151
Patriot's Point Naval and Maritime Museum, 129
Patrons of Husbandry (see Grange), 90, 95
Patterson, Elizabeth, 133
Payne, Daniel A., 68, 71, 85
Peace Center for the Performing Arts, 136
Peace of Paris, 49
Peach Island, 51
Pee Dee, 25, 106

pellagra, 99
Pelzer Manufacturing Company, 94
Pelzer, Francis, 94
Pendleton District, 62, 67
Pendleton Farmers' Society, 62
Pendleton Messenger, 69
Pendleton, Nathaniel, 33
Penn Normal and Industrial School, 84
Pennsylvania, 9, 24, 74
People's State Bank, 111
Perquimans County, 13
Perry, Benjamin F., 87
Perry, James M. "Miss Jim," 106
Perry, Matthew J., 130
Peterkin, Julia, 110
Petigru, James L., 77
Philadelphia, Pennsylvania, 27, 40, 41, 51, 55, 56, 63, 64
Phoenix Riot, 101
phosphate, 88
Pickens County, 42, 67, 89, 91, 117
Pickens, Andrew, 33, 43
Pierce, Franklin, 77
Pinckney (ship), 146
Pinckney, Charles, 33, 38, 50, 51, 57, 63
Pinkney, Charles Cotesworth, 33, 51, 56, 57, 59, 60
Pinckney, Clementa, 150
Pinckney, Eliza Lucas, 27
Pinckney, Henry Laurens, 71
Pinckney, Thomas, 56
Pinckney, William, 146
Pitt, William (statue), 37
Plan of Regulation, 35
Planter (ship), 84
Plessy v. Ferguson, 100, 101
Poe, Edgar Allan, 67
Poetry Society, 108
Poinsett, Joel R., 66
poinsettia, 66, 67
Polk, James K., 74
John Paul II (pope), 134
Pope, Joseph D., 94
Porgy, 112
Porgy and Bess, 112, 126
Port Royal, 19

Port Royal (ship), 10
Port Royal County, 18
Port Royal Sound, 5, 10, 18, 83
Portugal/Portuguese, 2, 31
Post and Courier, 59, 150
Potter, Edward, 86
Pottersville, 62
Presbyterians, 12
Presidential Medal of Freedom, 138
Prevost, Augustine, 44
Prince Frederick Parish, 24, 30
Prince George Winyah Parish, 22, 24, 34
Prince of Tides, The, 133
Prince William Parish, 27
Pritchard, Paul, 57
Progressive Democratic Party, 115
Provincial Congress, 38, 39, 40, 41
PTL (Praise the Lord), 134
Pulaski, Casimir, 44
Pulitzer Prize, 110, 150
Purry, Jean Pierre, 24
Purrysburg, 24, 24

Quakers, 60
Queen Anne's War, 16

Rainey, Joseph H., 90
Ralph Johnson (ship), 152
Ramsay, David, 52, 60
Randolph (ship), 43
Ransier, Alonzo J., 90
Ravenel, Charles D. "Pug," 128
Rawdon, Francis, 47
Reagan, Ronald, 132, 133
Reconstruction, 80, 81,88, 105, 123, 136, 139, 149, 153
Reconstruction Era National Historic Park, 153
Reconstruction Era National Monument (*see* Reconstruction Era National Historical Park)
"The Recruiting Officer," 113
Reformed Society of Israelites, 66
Regulator Movement, 32, 34, 35, 36, 37
Republican Party, 92, 122, 123, 128, 131, 139, 142

Revised Statutes of South Carolina, 91
Revolution of 1719, 20
Revolution of 1890, 96
Rhett, Robert Barnwell, 74, 75
Rhett, William, 17, 20
Ribaut, Jean, 5
Rice: cultivation, 9, 11, 13, 49, 104; export, 10, 17, 23, 40
Rice, Tom, 149
Richardson, Richard, 40
Richland County, 50
Ridgeville, 153
rifle clubs, 92
Riley, Joseph P., Jr., 129, 132
Riley, Richard, 131, 132, 137
Riverbanks Zoo, 128
Rivers Bridge (Battle of), 86
Riviera Theater, 114
Roanoke River, 1
Robert, Henry Martyn, 92
Robert's Rules of Order, 92
Robinson, Jackie, 121
Rock Hill, 98, 105, 121, 129
Rocky Mount, 58
Rogers, George, 131
Rogers, George C., Jr., 140
Rogers, Moses, 63
Romney, Mitt, 149
Roosevelt, Franklin Delano, 99, 111, 112, 113, 114, 115, 116
Roosevelt, Theodore, 102, 103, 104
Rose Bud, or Youth's Gazette, The, 69
Round O, 48
Royal, C. C., 128
Royal Council, 22, 31, 36
"Runnin' Wild," 109
Russell, Donald S., 122
Rutledge, Edward, 38, 41, 43, 44, 51, 52, 53
Rutledge, John, 33, 38, 41, 42

St. Andrew's Parish, 17, 20
St. Andrew's Society, 23
St. Augustine, Florida, 5, 6, 11, 16, 23, 26, 44, 46
St. Bartholomew's Parish, 17, 77
St. Cecilia Society, 34

St. David's Parish, 35

St. Finbar's Cathedral, (Ireland), 64

St. George's Dorchester Parish, 20

St. Helena Island, 84

St. Helena's Parish, 19, 34

St. James's Goose Creek Parish, 17

St. James's Santee Parish, 17, 22, 29

St. John's Berkeley Parish, 17

St. John's Colleton Parish, 24

St. John's River, 5, 26

St. Luke's Parish, 34, 74

St. Mark's Parish, 30

St. Mark's Episcopal Church, 87

St. Mary's Catholic Church, 30

St. Matthew's Parish, 65

St. Michael's Church (Charleston), 12, 29, 30, 57

St. Michael's Parish, 28

St. Paul's Parish, 17, 24, 31

St. Peter's Parish

St. Philip's Church (Charleston), 12, 22, 26, 56

St. Philip's Parish, 28

St. Stephen's Parish, 29

St. Thomas's and St. Denis's Parish, 17

Salazar, Pedro de, 3

Salkehatchie River, 86

Saluda County, 100

Saluda Manufacturing Company, 70

Saluda River, 94

Sampit River, 23

San Miguel de Gualdape, 4

Sandford, Robert, 7

Sanford, Mark, 147, 149

Santa Elena, 5, 6

Santee Canal Company, 50

Santee-Cooper, 112, 114, 115, 132, 147, 152

Santee River, 3, 47, 48, 50, 51

Santo Domingo, 3, 4, 54

Sardoine (ship), 34

Savannah (ship), 63

Savannah River, 1, 2, 3, 4, 18, 24, 39, 118, 136

Savannah River plant, 118, 145, 153

Savannah, Georgia, 24, 44, 55, 86

Saxe-Gotha, 25

Saxton, Rufus, 86

Sayle, William, 10

SCANA Corporation, 153

Scarlet Sister Mary, 110

SCE&G (South Carolina Electric and Gas), 143, 147

Scots, 12, 13, 17, 23

Scott, Robert K., 88, 89

Scott, Tim, 149, 150

Scott, Winfield, 77, 93

Screven, Elisha, 23

Seamen's Acts, 65, 66, 74

Secession, 76, 77, 80, 82

Secession Convention, 82, 83

Secessionville (Battle of), 84

Second Military District, 88

Seminoles, 82

Seoul, South Korea, 131

September 11th, 145

787 Dreamliner, 148

Seven Years' War (*see* French and Indian War)

Seymore, Horatio, 89

Shannon, W. M., 91

Shaw, Robert Gould, 85

Shawnees, 19

"Shell Manifesto," 96

Sherman, William Tecumseh, 80, 85, 86

Shute's Folly, 55

Sickles, Daniel E., 87, 88

Simms, William Gilmore, 54, 71

Simons, Benjamin, 15

single member election districts, 124, 128

Singleton, Richard, 72

Siouan, 2

sit-ins, 138

6-0-1 school law, 109

slave rebellion, 4, 40, 54, 62, 65, 75

slavery, 14, 26, 53, 54, 60, 64, 71, 72, 74, 80, 83, 87, 153; laws, 14, 15, 21, 26, 58, 64

slaves (*see* enslaved people)

Slidell, John, 83

Sloane, Hans, 77

Smalle, Reuben, 77

smallpox, 25, 30, 82

Smalls, Robert, 84, 87

Smith v Allwright, 116

Smith, Alfred E., 110
Smith, Ellison Durant ("Cotton Ed"), 103
Smith, James W., 90
Smith, Robert, 56
Smith, Susan, 139
Smith, Thomas, 22
Smith, William Loughton, 33
Smyth, Ellison, 94
Snow Campaign, 40
Social Security Act, 113
Society for the Preservation of Old Dwell-
    ings, 108
Society for the Propagation of Christian
    Knowledge, 15
Society for the Propagation of the Gospel
    in Foreign Parts, 16
Society of the Cincinnati, 49
Society of the Daughters of the American
    Revolution, 96
Solomon, James L., 122
Sonoco Products, 101
Sons of Liberty, 59
Sothell, Seth, 14
Soto, Hernado de, 4
South Carolina (ship), 45
South Carolina Academy of Fine Arts, 64
South Carolina Aquarium, 144
South Carolina Athletic Hall of Fame, 108
South Carolina Baptist Convention, 77,
    137
South Carolina Bar, 129
South Carolina Bar Association, 67, 94,
    129
South Carolina Canal and Rail Road
    Company, 50, 67
South Carolina College (see University of
    South Carolina)
South Carolina Constitution (1776), 41
South Carolina Constitution (1778), 42,
    43
South Carolina Constitution (1790), 52,
    54, 60, 61, 62, 85
South Carolina Constitution (1865), 87
South Carolina Constitution (1868), 89
South Carolina Constitution (1895), 98,
    117, 119, 124, 127, 141, 147

South Carolina Cotton Manufactory, 62
South Carolina Educational Television
    (SCETV), 120
South Carolina Federation of Colored
    Women's Clubs, 104
South Carolina Golf Club, 51
South Carolina Governor's School for the
    Arts, 131
South Carolina Governor's School for
    Science and Mathematics, 134
South Carolina Grand Council, 10, 14
South Carolina Hall of Fame, 127
South Carolina Historical Society, 77
South Carolina Homespun Company, 60
South Carolina Legislative Black Caucus,
    123, 128
South Carolina Military Academy, 73
South Carolina National Bank, 136
South Carolina Navy, 43
South Carolina Penitentiary, 88, 113
South Carolina Philharmonic Orchestra,
    119
South Carolina Public Welfare Act, 113
South Carolina Society, 28
South Carolina Society for Promoting and
    Improving Agriculture and Other Rural
    Concerns, 50
South Carolina State University, 125
South Carolina Supreme Court, 90, 133,
    134, 138, 141
South Caroliniana Library, 73
South Caroliniana Society, 113
South Edisto River, 6
South-Carolina Gazette, 24, 26, 40
"Southern Charm," 150
Southern Continental Army, 46
Southern Rights Association, 76
southern strategy, 131
Spain/Spanish, 2, 3, 4, 11, 13, 15, 16, 17, 23,
    27, 101
Spanish-American War, 101
Spartan District, 45
Spartanburg, 50, 73, 76, 88, 95, 106, 110,
    130, 138
Spartanburg County, 50, 112
Special Field Order No. 15, 86

Spoleto Festival, 129
Springs Industries, 139
Stamp Act, 33, 34, 37
Stamp Act Congress, 33
Star of the West (ship), 82
State Agricultural and Mechanical Society,
    95
State Bank, 58
State Board of Charities and Corrections,
    105
State Board of Health, 93
State Board of Law Examiners, 104
State Budget and Control Board, 118, 151
State College for Negroes at Orangeburg
    (see South Carolina State University)
State Department of Parks, Recreation,
    and Tourism, 125
State Fair, 78, 127
State Forestry Commission, 109
State Gazette of South-Carolina, 49
State Highway Department, 106, 112
State House: Charleston, 29; Columbia,
    51, 77, 92, 121
State Museum, 97, 134
State Planning Board, 113
State Ports Authority, 115
State Railroad Commission, 93
State Tax Commission, 105
State-Record Company, 133
Stephens, Alexander, 91
Stevenson v. West, 128
Stevenson, Adlai, 119, 120
Stevenson, Nancy, 130
Stono Rebellion, 26, 44
Stono River, 26, 44
Stuart, J. E. B., 85
Stuart, John, 31
Stuart's Town, 13
Sullivan's Island, 41, 57, 67
Summerville High School, 146
Sumner, Charles. 78
Sumter County, 102
Sumter, Thomas, 33, 45, 46, 47
Super Sofa store fire, 147
Swamp Angel, 85
Swinton, William, 23

Swiss, 24
sword of state, 17

Taft, William H., 103, 104
Talley, James, 138
Tamar (ship), 40
Tampico, Mexico, 75
Tariff of 1828, 69
Tariff of 1832, 69
Tariff of 1833, 69
Tarleton, Banastre, 44, 45, 48
Taxpayers Convention, 90, 91
Taylor, James, 50
Taylor, Thomas, 50
Taylor, Zachary75
TD Arena, 150
Tea Act, 38
Teach, Edward (see Thatch, Edward)
telegraph, 75
Tennent, William, 40
Tennessee River, 4
Texas, 53
Thatch, Edward, 20
The Big Chill, 132
The Code of Honor, 72
The Negro Law of South Carolina, 75
The Patriot, 144
The Southern Review, 67
The State, 151
The Statutes at Large of South Carolina, 71
Theodora (ship), 83
Thirteenth Amendment, 87
Thomas, Samuel, 16
Thompson, William, 41
Three Brothers (ship), 10
Thurmond, Strom, 116, 117, 119, 122, 123, 138,
    139, 140, 141, 142, 145, 146
Tilden, Samuel, 92, 95, 96, 98, 102
Tillman, Benjamin Ryan, 81, 95, 96, 98, 102
Tillman, James H., 102
Timothy, Ann, 25
Timothy, Ann Donovan, 49
Timothy, Lewis, 25, 26
Timrod, Henry, 104
Toal, Jean Hoefer, 134, 141
tobacco, 11, 65, 141

Tokyo, Japan, 115
Topper Site, 2
tornadoes, 114, 132
Tower of London, 46
Town Theater, 107
Towne, Laura, 84
Townes, Charles, 122
Townshend duties, 36
Township Auditorium, 117
Travel + Leisure, 151
Treadwell, Henrie Montieth, 122
Treaty of Augusta, 31
Treaty of DeWitt's Corner, 42
Treaty of Madrid, 11
Treaty of Paris (1763), 31
Trott, Nicholas, 19, 25
Trump, Donald, 151
Tubman, Harriet, 84
Turnbull, Robert J., 69
Tuscarora, 18, 19
Twenty-First Amendment, 111
Tyger River, 48
Tyler, John, 74

Union Camp Corporation, 132
Union County, 50
United Nations, 152
United States Constitution, 33, 51, 60, 65,
    68, 70
United States House of Representatives,
    60, 71, 74, 97, 133, 147; speaker, 62, 78
United States Interior Department, 129
United States Marine Corps, 96
United States Military Academy, 90
United States Naval Academy, 91
United States Senate, 56, 59, 62, 67, 70, 72,
    76, 78, 80, 96, 98, 99, 102, 103, 111, 113, 119,
    145, 146, 149, 150
United States Supreme Court, 56, 59, 99,
    100, 111, 115, 116, 119, 126, 128, 136, 144, 153
United Textile Workers (A. F. of L.), 112
University of South Carolina, 54, 58, 63,
    67, 71, 73, 75, 91, 92, 94, 98, 100, 122, 126,
    131, 136, 140, 145, 148, 149, 152
University of South Carolina Press, 105
US Air Flight 1016, 138

V.C. Summer Nuclear Generating Station,
    122, 147, 152
Van Buren, Angelica Singleton, 72
Van Buren, Martin, 72, 73, 75
Vaughn, Joseph A., 124
Verrazzano, Giovanni de, 4
Vesey, Denmark, 65
Vesey, Robert, 87
video poker, 141
Vietnam, 146, 152
Virginia, 7, 9, 31, 45, 46, 48, 78, 86
Volvo, 145, 153
Voorhees Normal and Industrial School,
    100
Voorhees, Ralph. 100
Voting Rights Act of 1965, 100, 124

Wachovia Bank, 136
Waddel, Moses, 59
Wagener, John A., 75
Walker, N. P., 73
Wallace, David Duncan, 112
Wallace, George, 126
Wando River, 17
War of 1812, 53, 61
War of Austrian Succession (*see* King
    George's War)
Waring, Waites, 117
Warren Lasch Conservation Center, 144
Washington, DC, 62, 68, 87, 142
Washington, Essie Mae, 141
Washington, George, 52, 56
Washington, William, 44
Water Company, 57
Wateree River, 3, 4
Water is Wide, The, 127
Waxhaws, 45
WCOS-TV, 119
"We Shall Overcome" (*see* "I'll Overcome
    Some Day")
Weatherly, Shawn, 131
Weaver, James B., 96
Weaver, Philip, 62
Webster, Daniel, 68, 75
Weld, Theodore, 72
Welsh, 25

Welsh Tract, 25
Wesley, John, 25
West Columbia, 8
West, Joseph, 8
Westinghouse Electric, 146
Westmoreland, William, 147
Westos, 11
Whig Party, 72
White Meeting House, 12
White Point, 20
Whitefield, George, 26
Whitmarsh, Thomas, 24
Whitney, Eli, 55
Who Speaks for the South?, 122
Wilkes, John, 36
William & Ralph (ship), 11
Williams, David R., 61
Williamsburg County, 50, 95
Williamson, Andrew, 40, 41
Williamson's Plantation, 45
Willington Academy, 59
Willkie, Wendell, 144
Wilmot Proviso, 74
Wilmot, David, 74
Wilson, Addison Graves "Joe," 148
Wilson, John Lyde, 72
Wilson, Woodrow, 104
Wilton, Joseph, 37
Wimbledon, 120
Winnsboro, 49, 144, 145
Winston-Salem, North Carolina, 136
Winthrop Normal College for Women
    (*see* Winthrop University)
Winthrop University, 98
Winton County (*see* Edgefield County)
Winyah Indigo Society, 29
Wirt, William, 69
Wofford College, 76, 95

Wofford, Benjamin, 76
Wofford, William, 38
Women's Christian Temperance Union, 93
Women's Issues Caucus, 137
Women's Medical College of Pennsylva-
    nia, 101
Woodland Period, 2
Woodmason, Charles, 34
Woodside, John T., 109
Woodward, Henry, 4
Workman, William D., 122
Works Progress Administration (WPA),
    113
World Boxing Association, 125
World War I, 106, 107
World War II, 99, 114, 116, 146
Wright, Elizabeth Evelyn, 100
Wright, Jonathan Jasper, 90
writ of habeas corpus, 91
WSPA-Spartanburg, 110

XYZ Affair, 56, 57

Yamacraw Bluff, 24
Yarmouth (ship), 43
Yawkey, Thomas A., 129
Yeamans, John, 7
Yeamans, William, 7
yellow fever, 15, 17
yellow Jessamine, 109
Yemassee, 17, 19, 20
Yemassee, The, 71
Yemassee War, 17, 19, 20
York County, 50, 128, 134, 143
York District, 73
Yorktown, 47
Yorktown (ship), 129
Young, Virginia Durant, 101